ULTRALUXE HOTELS

THE EXPERIENCE AWAITS...

John Wiley & Sons, Ltd

2021002150

Published in Great Britain in 2009 by John Wiley & Sons Ltd
The Atrium, Southern Gate, Chichester.
West Sussex PO19 8SQ, England
Telephone +44 (0)1243 779777

Email (for orders and customer service enquiries): cs-books@wiley.co.uk

Visit our Home Page on www.wiley.com

Other Wiley Editorial Offices

John Wiley & Sons Inc., 111 River Street, Hoboken, NJ 07030, USA

Jossey-Bass, 989 Market Street, San Francisco, CA 94103-1741, USA

Wiley-VCH Verlag GmbH, Boschstr. 12, D-69469 Weinheim, Germany

John Wiley & Sons Australia Ltd, 42 McDougall Street, Milton, Queensland 4064, Australia

John Wiley & Sons (Asia) Pte Ltd, 2 Clementi Loop #02-01, Jin Xing Distripark, Singapore 129809

John Wiley & Sons Canada Ltd, 5353 Dundas Street West, Suite 400, Etobicoke, Ontario M9B 6H8, Canada

Wiley also publishes its books in a variety of electronic formats. Some content that appears in print may not be
available in electronic books.

Editor: Mariangela Palazzi-Williams

Art Director: Roberto Di Filitto, Spazio8, www.spazio8.com

Page layout: Nathalie Schneider

ISBN 9780470759011

Printed by Everbest, China

ULTRALUXE HOTELS

THE EXPERIENCE AWAITS...

Veronica Newson

Editor Mariangela Palazzi-Williams
Art Director Roberto di Filitto, Spazio8

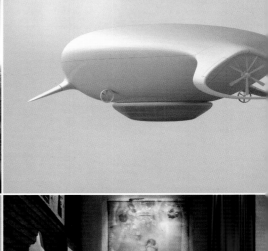

CONTENTS

Introduction

A great hotel is not just a building;
it's an individual, with personality, spirit and authenticity.

A comment on Gramercy Park Hotel, New York, these words go to the very heart of what for me is ultraluxe. In my work as a specialist travel consultant I come across a host of 'experiences' and these pages showcase the places where I'd really like to stay. Of course, many of them provide luxury at prices to match, but many are here because they offer not only great hospitality but something else, something truly original. The things that catch my eye are beautiful buildings, eclectic furniture and fittings by modern designers, carefully chosen antiques, an innovative use of lighting, thoughtful environmentally sensitive touches. I want to take you on a virtual journey that criss-crosses the globe from East to West and, I hope, has a destination for every taste. Here are paradise island hideaways and old world European elegance, colonial safari lodges and urban retreats... Here we focus on the brand new and newly renovated, paying special attention to the most recent Asian destinations in China, Bhutan and Vietnam....

Much space is devoted to the stunning photography while the text seeks to convey that bit of extra magic that enhances a guest's stay, whether it is the breathtaking views, the offerings of a virtuoso chef or the sublime decor of the spa.

Ultimately, this is my personal selection and others would come up with a very different list. But there is no right or wrong way to do ultraluxe. These are my recommendations and I am happy to share them with you.

Veronica Newson

From left to right: Relaxation in the lounge and in the bedroom at Blake and in the lounge at Haymarket Hotel; butler service round the clock at Town House Galleria; patisserie perfection at Mandarin Oriental Tokyo.

THE LUXURY HOSPITALITY MARKET

Competition at the top end of the hospitality market is fierce – and is very much in the guests' interest. The hotel choice has become a global lifestyle issue, and perhaps not before time. Nowadays travellers are not just concerned with convenience of location, level of service at reception and size of bedrooms. Instead, what counts is the overall 'experience', a magical word that encompasses just about everything, from the look of the place to the attentiveness of the concierge, from the cachet of the chef and the atmosphere at the bar to the crowd it attracts, from the places of interest in the vicinity to the range of treatments available at the spa, from the signature toiletries to the state-of-the-art gym...

Traditionally two types of hotel respond to the needs of the more discerning leisure tourists looking for luxury. First there are the elite hotel groups with an established and growing global reach and a portfolio of world famous 'trophy' hotels: St Regis, Ritz-Carlton, Hyatt, Kempinski, Kingdom, Jumeirah and Taj Hotels. Despite the individuality of each location, these collections can guarantee a worldwide uniformly excellent experience in all their hotels. Mandarin Oriental's spiritual essence and attention to detail, for example, are carried through in every one of their hotels and envied the world over.

Starwood Hotel's Luxury Collection upholds a standard and service benchmark rigorously maintained and offered across a wide range of destinations, each handpicked and continually subject to review. Such hotels are usually preferred by the more mature traveller, for whom luxury, attention to detail, fine food and wine, state-of-the-art spas and gyms and, of course, unparalleled service are paramount.

The second type of hotel operating in this market belongs to the likes of Thompson Hotels and Firmdale Hotels, that created a modern, design-led response to the more traditional luxury premises of the first category, introducing the so called 'boutique or collection hotels'.

A pioneer in the boutique hotel field, Anouska Hempel, opened Blakes in 1978, followed by the Dylan Hotel in Amsterdam and The Hempel in London. Most recently Hempel has designed Warapuru, a luxurious eco-resort in Aztec style set in the Brazilian rainforest with its own private beach. With 40 individual pavilions, a beach club restaurant and a state-of-the-art spa are being built in Itacare, Bahia, Brazil, due to open 2009.

Based in the UK with a portfolio of six London hotels, the interior design for each Firmdale venture has been created by Kit Kemp in a fresh, contemporary English style, thoughtfully combining colour and texture, modern touches and antique pieces. Firmdale Hotels also play host to an enviable art collection, a combination that has proved so successful with the Haymarket and Townhouse in London that they have decided to venture into New York's SoHo with The Crosby Street Hotel (due to open in 2009).

Thompson Hotels' accent is on timeless standards and avant-garde style: a small cluster of nine hotels exists in the USA and a tenth is scheduled to open in Toronto in 2009. Complemented by the group customary luxury touches, sophisticated design and trademark 24-hour concierge service, Thompson Toronto will also have a rooftop pool and bar overlooking the city's eclectic fashion and design district.

FASHION HOTELS

Beside the usual business players, the luxury hotel market has recently attracted new partnerships with celebrities who are brands in themselves or have a global reputation such as sports personalities, international actors and chefs, fashion designers and retail brands.

Among the more exuberant examples are the two Parisian creations by Christian Lacroix. Hôtel du Petit Moulin, in the Marais, welcomes guests to an exotic world of bohemian luxury with 17 individually conceived rooms, while the new Hôtel Bellechasse, in Faubourg St Germain, draws on the genteel inhabitants of the area, its museums and antique emporia to offer 34 extravagant yet elegant guestrooms. Here photo-transfer collages taken from motifs of classical sculptures and elements from old engravings blend with a rich palette of textures and colours, silk-Jacquard upholstered chairs, macassar-wood doors and jewel-toned faux leather on the walls.

A high profile fashion business, Bulgari started its hospitality adventure in Milan, with a sophisticated signature hotel realised in whites, cream and browns in the form of dark teak woods in a very clean and contemporary design. The Bulgari Suite has a Turkish Bihara stone bath and stone block fireplace. It extends onto the teak terrace with views over the gardens or local villas. Bulgari Resort in Bali is set on a 160-metre high cliff overlooking the ocean and draws its inspiration from an eclectic mix of traditional Balinese architecture and contemporary Italian design, using indigenous stone, native wood and local fabrics exclusively created for Bulgari. The Bulgari Villa has 24-hour service and a private 20-metre lap pool.

From left to right: Peace and freedom at Tuckers Point, Capella Pedregal and Mondrian; ultraluxe features and impeccable service at Burj al Arab, Town House Galleria and Marques de Riscal.

Giorgio Armani has also been busy in the hotel arena, working in close collaboration with Emaar and creating Armani Hotels and Resorts. The first venture will open in Dubai in 2009 where it will be located in the highest building in the world, the Burj Tower. It will feature 160 guest rooms and suites, a spa, a club and a selection of restaurants and will be complemented by 144 Armani Residences, each with the personal Armani touch.

Actors, chefs and sports stars have also diversified into the niche hotel business. Tiger Woods, for example, is behind an exclusive lifestyle community at the spectacular Al Ruwaya Golf Course. Tiger Woods Dubai is envisaged as an oasis of luxury within the proposed luxury boutique hotel, spa destination and golfers' Middle Eastern paradise with golf academy and state-of-the-art clubhouse, its golfing community living in the 22 palaces, 75 mansions and 100 luxury villas dotted around the estate. In Europe, Gordon Ramsay has recently announced the purchase of The York & Albany near Regent's Park in London as a gourmet dining destination. Earmarked for opening in late 2009, it will accommodate two restaurants, a deli, private dining areas and a huge bar with designer guestrooms upstairs.

In Latin America, film director Francis Ford Coppola has purchased and developed three hotels – Blancaneaux Lodge in the jungle of Belize and Turtle Inn on the coast, and La Lancha across the border in Guatemala. A regular visitor to all his properties, he is sometimes to be found cooking in the restaurant when he is not poring over the latest script and plans for a movie.

Brad Pitt, GRAFT and Zabeel Properties have recently come together in a new collaboration to launch Dubai's first green and sustainable hotel and resort project with an American theme. The 800-room five-star ambitious initiative is being designed to host the most glamorous events and award ceremonies in the near future and the team are actively striving for a minimum of gold status LEED (Leadership in Energy and Environmental Design).

EVERYBODY CAN BE A HOTELIER

However, the list doesn't end there. New developments in the real estate arena and new financial solutions have recently blurred the line between guest and owner, bringing the hotel experience into the guest's private life, in more ways than ever previously imagined.

Micro-ownership, for example, is an attractive option for would-be hoteliers. According to this solution an expensive asset like a hotel, a destination club or experience club can be divided into shares which can be sold to individual owners for a relative percentage use of the asset.

The benchmark in this area is currently the St Regis Residence Club, which scored highly in terms of guest satisfaction, social status, brand exclusivity and the provision of unrivalled service and amenities according to a recent survey.

New players are moving in fast, though, like Mondrian South Beach Hotel Residences by innovative Dutch designer Marcel Wanders in the style of 'Sleeping Beauty's castle' in the up and coming neighbourhood of Biscayne Bay, Florida. Here guests step into a magical world of garden oases conceived as indoor and outdoor living spaces with an outdoor bar and a glistening chandelier suspended above a glorious pool. The main building is curvilinear and extends to form a semicircular sculptural structure in which the rooms resemble theatre boxes and overlook the gardens below giving each guest 'the best seat in the house'. Here the residences are loft-like spaces, flooded with natural light flowing uninterrupted between the living areas and balanced by dark wood flooring throughout. This prime waterfront property has views of the bay, ocean and downtown. There are 342 studios, one and two-bedroom apartments and penthouses decorated in a sophisticated colour palette of white, gold, brown, grey, blue and black. Mondrian South Beach facilities will include an Agua spa, a world-class restaurant, a vibrant and dynamic nightlife experience, and a 40-slip marina with private dock master.

Another example in the mould is the Tucker's Point Private Club and Residential Community in Bermuda, the island's most exclusive resort. Located in Tucker's Town and situated on 200 acres of privately owned waterfront land in Bermuda, it is next to the Mid Ocean Club and offers breathtaking views of Castle Harbour, Harrington Sound and the Atlantic Ocean. This $350 million investment will have a luxury resort of 88 spacious guestrooms and a world class spa, due to open in April 2009. An 18-hole Roger Rulewich-designed golf course and clubhouse, four Har-Tru clay tennis courts and a Beach Club with access to a private pink sand beach, freshwater 'horizon' swimming pool and water sports centre will all feature.

In Mexico Capella Pedregal is accessed by a private mountain tunnel from downtown Cabo San Lucas, Baja, where aside from the 66-room Capella Resort and Spa, there will be 31 shared-ownership Capella Residences and 20 full-ownership Capella Casonas, all with dramatic views of the Pacific Ocean and the Sea of Cortez. The resort is located close to the world-class Cabo Marina and access to 61-foot luxury Viking yachts at the Capella Pedregal Yacht Club. The highlight of the complex is the sea-to-summit Auriga Spa designed by Sylvia Sepielli, renowned for drawing on native cultures to inspire spa treatments and rituals.

THE ULTRALUXE MARKET

With so many key players in the luxury market, the lines are starting to blur between the larger groups, the niche collections and the independents, as the desire to continue the quest for the unusual and fantastic gathers pace.

So just what is it that sets the exclusive luxury hotels apart? At the heart of a true premium hotel is the move towards maintaining an ultraluxe experience not only within the hotel but also beyond, such that the hotel becomes an extension of a guest's life, their needs and expectations continually recorded and updated and used to build the relationship and enhance the experience.

Ultraluxe hotels aim to provide nothing but the very best, adding those intangible elements that make the experience really memorable. Here guests receive an extraordinary level of attention, as if they alone were the only thing that mattered.

A few years ago the first seven-star hotel, Burj Al Arab, raised the stakes with its astonishing welcome reception and awe-inspiring atrium lobby, personal receptions on each floor, a minimum of a duplex suite for each guest, a helipad, fleet of Rolls Royce, Bentley and other limousines and sports cars to play with and an underwater restaurant and several more dining choices on site.

With the Burj Al Arab as a benchmark, the rest were challenged to provide equal luxury – there was no room for failure. Some things could be anticipated – attentive, personalised service and exclusivity are the bare minimum. Other ingredients could be provided by teams of butlers and concierge who are the hotel's life-blood, ensuring that guests are happy and keep coming back, confident in the knowledge that their comfort is the hotel's primary concern and reassured by 'essential extras' such as sleep menus, anti-snoring pillows and bath butlers... Nowadays there are even tanning butlers to achieve the 'perfect' tan. The Mandarin Oriental's Amber restaurant in Hong Kong has a dedicated hot-chocolate sommelier to recommend the best accompaniment to a dessert and prepare customised drinks. If a guest asks for a helicopter for a ride over Central Park, they will probably get one. Demand for such services has never been greater and new models of 'luxury' are continually evolving.

THE RISE OF THE CONCIERGE

New guests at such hotels can expect to be contacted in advance and invited to specify likes and dislikes, food and flower preferences and any other special requests. At the hotel, the once tiresome process of checking-in now happens in a more casual and intimate environment, with paperwork completed in the room, in a suite, by an open

air pond with a cocktail in hand or over a cup of tea.

The role of the concierge has expanded beyond recognition and hotel concierge programmes are becoming more widespread. Hyatt has 'e-concierge' linking guests to concierges to book local activities and restaurants before they arrive. Loews has its 'In the know' programme whereby concierges put together a list of local events and happenings and share them with front-desk staff and porters who pass the information on to guests.

Sometimes it is the simple things that count. The Ritz-Carlton hotel in New York's Battery Park has a concierge team that never forgets guests' names, remembers most guests' breakfast preferences and never bats an eyelid when a guest asks to purchase the bed linen or even the bed. Highly skilled butlers are available, trained to repair every type of gadget in a crisis. The team has even been called upon to organise a private dining experience with a fireworks display set off at a key time over the Statue of Liberty in support of a business proposal. Guests keep in touch with their concierge and use them as an adjunct to their office and private lives – the relationship just keeps on growing.

ARCHITECTURE, ART AND DESIGN

Together with the level of service, the decor is also key to the enjoyment of the stay. This thinking is behind the success of the range of more intimate boutique and design hotels. Since the 1970s, when Anouska Hempel launched Blakes in London and Ian Schrager, Steve Rubell with Andrée Putman created Morgans Hotel in New York, this boutique sector, according to sources in 2007, has been worth somewhere between $6 billion and $7 billion a year globally.

In 1999, Starwood launched 'W' Hotels, described as a 'fun, hip and exciting hotel collection that happily marries boutique hotel flair with the quality and functionality of larger brand hotels'.

Ian Schrager, one of the master innovators of the hip and boutique hotel and Bill Marriott Jr. of Marriott, the biggest hotel chain in the world, met in 2007 to develop an idea for 'a new style of boutique hotel'. Based on the next generation, which Schrager has recently pioneered with the Gramercy Park Hotel, here first class service and amenities are now complemented by exclusive works of art, cultural references and high end design.

Moving up and onwards, arresting architecture and cutting-edge design are indeed

From left to right: Location, location, location at the Royal Olympic in Athens and more luxurious touches at Le Cigale in Qatar, both with lighting by Nord Light; small details make all the difference at Trump; green tourism has exploded: Orchard Garden Hotel, San Francisco, and Azura, Mozambique; space travel with Virgin Galactic.

worth a fortune in many cases. Take the Four Seasons Hotel Ty Warner Penthouse in New York, happy to charge its guests premium rates for the privilege of enjoying the breathtaking triumph of architecture achieved by IM Pei and the extravagant and stunning interiors by interior architect Peter Marino, all complemented by bird's eye views of the city that never sleeps.

LOCATION, LOCATION, LOCATION

Just as valuable as the investment in interiors and the level of service, a hotel's location plays a key part in the overall experience. Access to culture, gourmet dining and shopping are key motivators in choice of destination. The city of Milan is a perfect example with Town House Galleria statement hotel right above Prada in the Galleria and the Presidential Suite at the Principe di Savoia, with its Pompeian-style private pool. Each of these hotels is ideally located for an evening at La Scala, a visit to the Duomo and for viewing Leonardo da Vinci's *Last Supper*, as well as for hitting the boutiques or being pampered.

The view can also be instrumental in selecting premium suites in a five star hotel, such as La Belle Étoile at Hotel Le Meurice, with its wide private terrace overlooking Paris. Similarly, the Royal Olympic hotel in Athens is blessed with the sight of the Temple of Zeus.

For those for whom shopping is a key motivator Dubai is evolving into a key destination. Very shortly, The World (a man-made archipelago off the coast of Dubai) will be host to Isla Moda, a fashion hub and resort conceived as an entire 'city of fashion' which will showcase the world's major luxury and style brands. A number of themed residential villas, a personal concierge for guests and residents including a style concierge for clothing, perfumery, personal makeovers and a design concierge to create unique living environments with bespoke furnishings, art and technology are all planned.

CARING FOR BOTH BODY AND SOUL

Partly because of the desire to cater for guests' every need, partly because it makes good business sense to keep them on the premises as long as possible, all major luxury hotels now offer a spa experience.

Spa resorts have expanded from their historical niche as purveyors of cures, clean air and the health-giving benefits of 'taking the waters' to evolve into luxurious havens and retreats from the stresses of modern living. In some cases the spa even moves straight into the guestroom. Trump International Hotel and Tower Chicago have such spa suites, exclusive enclaves for guests serious about their health and their pampering. Nor is today's spa any longer the exclusive preserve of women; men are becoming regular attendees, enjoying treatments specifically designed for them. Spa rooms for two are the norm where couples can enjoy the same or concurrent treatments in each other's company.

The very notion of the spa has also evolved and in some instances has crossed over from the site of healthy living and holistic beauty therapies into a hybrid of clinic and spa, where terry towelling robes now happily rub shoulders with lab coats and medical professionals conduct serious programmes that run the gamut from botox and collagen injections, to orthopaedic procedures, to weight loss and detox, derma fills and microdermabrasions or chemical peels, through to post-operative and hotel-style support.

Lanserhof is a dedicated medical spa set in the Tyrol, Austria: its core philosophy is concerned with eating and digestion and guests learn to chew, savour and digest their food. It's a state-of-the-art medical centre and also runs programmes that address sleep disorders, menopausal symptoms, impotence, low energy and stress.

In terms of wellbeing tourist destinations, probably one of the most sought after weight loss or balance and detox options is Clínica Buchinger, in Marbella, which provides a doctor led programme with a very high success rate.

A most recent development from the spa experience is the world of medical tourism, where discretion and respect for personal privacy are paramount and hotels support guests in their physical and mental recovery. Clients for this kind of destination are those medical tourists who want to escape the cost and often dubious quality of surgery and hygiene on offer in their own country and are prepared to go abroad to address more serious physical conditions. Costa Rica stands out as having well-equipped, luxurious recovery retreats with hotel-style guest houses that cater specifically to post-operative patients. South Africa is excellent for cosmetic or addiction treatments away from the paparazzi; guests leave home for a 'month long safari' in order to undertake breast augmentation and liposuction procedures, knowing their privacy is guaranteed.

CLEAN CONSCIENCE: ECO AND ETHICAL TOURISM

Conservation, sustainable development and cultural preservation are now high on a rapidly growing number of agendas. As the green consumer is likely to be affluent and

professional, very little compromise on luxury is allowed. To cater for these guests, several luxury hotels now offer carbon offset programmes allowing travellers to redeem the amount of carbon dioxide generated by a given activity (e.g. their flight, transfer by car) by investing in a project to remove or prevent the equivalent amount of CO_2 being released into the atmosphere.

The Palazzo Las Vegas takes luxury to new heights with over 3,000 suites and an 85,000 square foot Barneys New York department store as its highlight. This $1.9 billion, 50-storey hotel is also the largest 'green' building in the world and was recently awarded the coveted Silver Leadership in Energy and Environmental Design certificate. Here recycled construction materials such as steel and concrete and solar power are only some of the features the carbon footprint of the hotel.

Orchard Garden Hotel in San Francisco leads the urban 'green boutique' revolution and is setting the standard for the boutique hotel that doesn't compromise on luxury. Azura at Gabriel's, Benjuerra Island, Mozambique, comprises 15 luxury villas constructed from sustainable sources and separated from each other by the Indian Ocean and by a private swimming pool and deck area. This eco-lodge has an active commitment to the local community: Azura's personnel is largely local and a development fund helps protect indigenous wildlife and woodland on the island as well as support the school and football team.

NEW DESTINATIONS, NEW LUXURY

Harrods now offers chocolates studded with Swarovski crystals with a price tag of £5,000 – a sign that, despite the overall economic slowdown in the West, there are still high spenders seeking the additional 'wow' factor. This also applies to the world of hospitality. Some Chinese capitalists, global hedge fund managers, footballers, Russian oligarchs, film stars and CEOs think nothing of reserving a hotel's presidential suite at $15,000 per night and their expectations are almost limitless in terms of luxury requirements: if they want to arrive by helicopter or private yacht, they will. The main beneficiaries of this new influx of rich tourists are relatively new destinations, in Africa, South America, the former Eastern bloc and the Far East, including some countries previously restricted for visitors.

More six and seven-star hotels are set to appear in these relatively new luxury destinations. Aman Resort has plans for such a hotel in northeast India in Orissa. A lush green state bounded by the Bay of Bengal, and as yet relatively undiscovered, it is a place of great natural beauty and imposing artefacts, surrounded by forested plateaus and coastal plains dotted with temples and historic monuments. Aman Resorts is also planning to renovate a number of ancient buildings near to Yíhé Yuán, the Garden of Harmonious Interests, at the Summer Palace in Beijing, a much loved and protected Unesco World Heritage site which may be converted into an exclusive luxury boutique hotel, underground spa, performance pavilion and club for patrons only. The Summer Palace is the largest and best-preserved imperial garden in China, formerly used by the country's imperial rulers as a retreat from the Forbidden City during the hottest months.

WHERE NEXT? THE SKY IS NO LONGER THE LIMIT

Consider Dubai once more, and the extraordinary lengths to which the country has innovated and literally expanded in recent years to embrace such extraordinary concepts as manmade private islands like Nakheel's The World. An artificial archipelago composed of 300 islands, the resort is surrounded by an oval breakwater off the coast of Dubai. Here an island will cost between $6 million and $250 million; currently 60 per cent have already been sold and buyers include a number of celebrities as well as developers. One developer is Jean van Gysel de Meise, owner of the luxurious five star Le Plaza in Brussels and the boutique brand V Vejer in Spain. Together with Italian designers Architetti Associati he has revealed plans to launch a luxurious V brand boutique on The World island of Greece with 65 hyper-luxurious living spaces using an environmentally conscious and sustainable approach that entails occupying only 37 per cent of the island to leave plenty of lush green gardens, wide open spaces and walkways.

How far can travellers go for new experiences? What is engaging the interest of today's global tourists and what are they looking forward to in the near future?

With such variety you might think there is no new direction left in which this market could diversify, but you would be wrong. Even as I write, its business entrepreneurs are rising to meet the challenge – in several cases quite literally. From 2009 Virgin Galactic's travellers will board a spacecraft and venture outside the Earth's atmosphere. Closer to the home planet, Manned Cloud, scheduled to be in operation by 2020, is an eco-friendly airship that will circumnavigate the globe offering spectacular views - and leaving no carbon footprint. And among projects presently in design is Apeiron, a futuristic architectural icon earmarked for the Gulf, whose guests will enjoy the amenities of a seven star hotel with everything built on water. Extraordinary innovation, breathtaking settings – ultraluxe experiences *par excellence.*

Out of this World

Where money is no object

Gramercy Park Hotel

New York, USA

A lifestyle revolution

The very name conjures up an era of glitz and glamour and evokes an ambience of times long gone, combined with 21st-century decor, flawless taste and discreet luxury – a world away from the New York of subways and diners, the noise of traffic and the bustling crowds. This is urban paradise.

A great hotel is not just a building it's an individual, with personality, spirit and authenticity'. Ian Schrager

www.gramercyparkhotel.com

Our recommendation
Custom Gramercy Suite from $2,200 per night
Deluxe Custom Gramercy Suite from $2,750 per night
The breathtaking Penthouse, price available on request

Best time to visit	**All year**
Design style	**A sensuous vision of aesthetic diversity**
Architects and designers	**Ian Schrager Company: Ian Schrager, Michael Overington and Anda Andrei in collaboration with friends including Maarten Baas and artist Julian Schnabel**

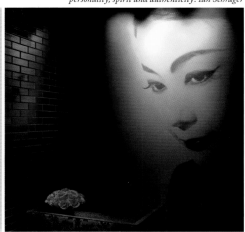

Chic after-hours supper on a private rooftop garden lit by an amazing ceiling installation.

Originally designed by Robert T Lyons, Gramercy Park Hotel was built by Bing and Bing in 1925 on the site of the former homes of flamboyant architect Stanford White and the controversial agnostic Robert Ingersoll.

This is the hotel that witnessed Humphrey Bogart's marriage to his first wife Helen Menken, embraced the Yankees' baseball legend Babe Ruth as a regular bar patron and welcomed writers, artists and musicians such as Bob Marley, The Clash and David Bowie as sometime residents.

Today, it is clear that Ian Schrager and his collaborators have successfully transformed this original bohemian into a bohemian original. Walking into the lobby is a theatrical feast for the eyes. 'Julian Schnabel's maximalist hand and Ian Schrager's minimalist choreography of style is a synergistic balancing act that always dances up to the edge of being too much without ever going over.'

The experience

The hotel provides the lavish backdrop to a truly remarkable collection of 20th century masterpieces by artists such as Richard Prince, Damien Hirst, Jean-Michel Basquiat, Andy Warhol and Julian Schnabel himself. The collection will rotate so that Gramercy's guest can enjoy an impressive range of works of art in what is an eclectic yet thoroughly relaxed environment.

The hotel boasts two of the hottest bars in New York, visually and culturally exciting and original spaces that manage to be both wildly eccentric and cutting-edge sophisticated at the same time. Candle-lit throughout, the Jade Bar represents a trip into the past and evokes the symbolic 'cocktail hour', inviting guests to order classic aperitifs at the bar.

The Rose Bar is an utterly bohemian reflection of an artist's studio with custom-designed furniture by Julian Schnabel and adorned with seductive works of art. Here, patrons can enjoy drinks and, if they wish, order from the hotel's acclaimed Wakiya Restaurant .

Overseen by Nobu Matsuhisa, and his Japanese chef Yuji Wakiya, the unique restaurant offers a new style of Chinese cooking inspired by the traditional

Julian Schnabel designed many of the extraordinary furniture and fixture pieces.

Jade Bar, evocative of the cocktail hour.

foods of Shanghai, Szechuan, Canton and Beijing – all recreated from a Japanese culinary perspective. The long, narrow dining room is opium-den chic, with tasseled curtains and satin sofas in raise-the-red-lantern red and black-pearl black. Wakiya dishes are beautifully presented works of art, a signature style reflected in their delicate arrangement. Wakiya also serves tasting portions so guests can enjoy variety from start to finish. He changes the menu to accommodate seasonally available ingredients, in order to harmonise the body with the effects of the season – summer vegetables, therefore, are believed to have a cooling effect on the body when the weather is hot. This yin/yang philosophy is applied throughout the menu, offering guests a superb culinary experience that is healthy and healing at the same time.

For your eyes only
Upstairs is the Private Roof Club and Garden, an area restricted to residents and select private members only. With a retractable roof over sumptuous gardens 16 storeys above the city, here are yet more works of art on which to feast the eyes including pieces by Andy Warhol and Damien Hirst, while the centrepiece is a truly breathtaking 'science-fiction' style chandelier. The garden is open for breakfast, business lunches, even intimate dinners;

alternatively this amazing venue can be reserved for late night cocktails.

The Aerospa is located on the same floor as this country club in the city and offers the very latest innovations in facials and whole body treatments for both men and women. Highlights include a jet-lag recovery massage and steam baths, as well as customised services.

The dynamic spirit of the public spaces is carried into each of the 185 unique, generously scaled and beautifully appointed guest rooms. The six custom suites express the Gramercy Park Hotel's singular vision and aesthetic anarchy. These are luxury private residences that embrace a Renaissance colour palette and are furnished with a distinctive collection of paintings and *objets d'art* gathered from around the world. Imported hand tufted rugs, velvet drapery, are juxtaposed with original creations by Julian Schnabel and Maarten Baas and blend together to create the perfect ambience.

The Penthouse has no equal. Renovated with custom plastered lime walls using a 600- year-old European technique and designed with a mahogany wood ceiling, an original Stanford White fireplace and mantle is beautifully set off by the arrangement of the furniture and decorations.

Private Roof Club.

Ty Warner Penthouse

Four Seasons Hotel, New York, USA

To stay here is to experience life within a sensational work of art

Situated between Park and Madison Avenues, the Four Seasons Hotel, New York, is the quintessential address from which to savour the city's vibrant culture and to stroll across Central Park. Staying in the Ty Warner Penthouse is to experience life as a work of art, to view the world below from your own miniature infinity pool while enjoying the services of a personal butler.

IM Pei's stunning architecture and Peter Marino's interiors combine to make this suite a breathtaking experience, perfectly complemented by the views over Manhattan.

www.fourseasons.com/newyorkfs

Our recommendation
Ty Warner Suite from $30,000 per night

Best time to visit	**All year** **The Ty Warner Penthouse is adored by a glittering guest list and is hard to book, so plan ahead**
Design style	**An art and design installation to live in**
Architects and designers	**IM Pei, architect and Peter Marino, interior architect**
Affiliation	**Four Seasons Hotels**

With floor-to-ceiling bay windows and glass balconies the Ty Warner Penthouse has the most breathtaking views of Manhattan.

In the palatial bathroom: Chinese onyx from ceiling to floor with hand-carved basins and an infinity bathtub for romantic evenings in.

Located in Manhattan's Four Seasons Hotel, New York, the Ty Warner Penthouse is the fruit of a collaboration between owner Ty Warner, Peter Marino and IM Pei, who was coaxed out of retirement to create this most opulent accommodation.

The Ty Warner Penthouse is accessed by its own private elevator. Once across the threshold, the guest has nine private rooms at their disposal in a setting that is truly stunning. Cantilevered glass balconies and floor-to-ceiling bay windows are set beneath 25-foot cathedral ceilings, framing the most breathtaking views of Manhattan and beyond.

To stay here is to experience life within a sensational work of art – every detail and furnishing in the Penthouse has been specially commissioned, from semi-precious stone surfaces to fabrics woven with platinum and gold. In the living and dining area, cream-coloured walls are inlaid with thousands of pieces of mother-of-pearl. A chandelier by Deborah Thomas sparkles above the bronze table by designer François-Xavier LaLanne, whose work is also found in the private library which hosts an enviable collection of books set in a bookcase framed with a beautiful vine leaf motif, illuminated by a chandelier.

The master bedroom boasts a Thai canopy bed threaded with gold. With its ceiling, walls and floor gleaming with onyx, the master bathroom encompasses a balcony overlooking Central Park.

The Penthouse also features a private spa room with a serene screen of living bamboo. Among the pampering features are a separate rain shower, an infinity-edge bathtub complete with chromatherapy, a separate glass-enclosed rain shower, radiant-heated floors, and sinks carved from a solid block of rock crystal. There is a therapist available to provide massage and treatments in situ.

As befits such splendid surroundings, Penthouse guests enjoy the services of both a personal butler and a personal trainer, while a private chauffeur is also available at any hour with either a Rolls Royce or Mercedes Maybach, according to preference, to take guests shopping, to the theatre, to JFK or wherever they wish in Manhattan.

Musha Cay at Copperfield Bay, a earthy paradise in the Bahamas.

Musha Cay at Copperfield Bay

Bahamas

A earthly paradise in the Bahamas

Set in the secluded Exuma Cays southeast of Nassau in the playground of the Bahamas, Musha Cay at Copperfield Bay is a private tropical heaven where the sea and the sky, the pleasure, the discrete service and all the amenities are yours to savour – and yours alone!

Only an illusionist of the calibre of David Copperfield could conjure such an earthly paradise for his guests, spoilt to the point that they can even dictate who else inhabits the island during their stay.

The most exclusive and expensive resort in the world, this sublime holiday destination is situated on its own island, dotted with palm trees and exotic flora and fauna. Spread over the eleven nearby Copperfield Bay islands are some forty private beaches, all available to guests, their glistening white sands lapped by the clear azure waters of the Caribbean.

Luxury, comfort and state of the art outdoor sports are the order of the day, with a free-form freshwater pool to relax in after a game of tennis and every imaginable boat and peace of water ski equipment made promptly available to surf the waters, including a 37 foot yacht and an inflatable Nautilus catamaran.

After sundown, entertainment switches back to the beach. At a torch-lit table romantically set at the water's edge, your personal chef will effortlessly magic freshly caught sea food or anything else that takes your fancy, all accompanied by the best vintages.

And when it is time for bed, let the sound of the ocean waves caressing your private beach lull you into a restful sleep, while you lie in one of only five guesthouses, surrounded by unique pieces of art collected from around the globe in a mix of traditional British colonial and colourful Bahamian styles.

www.mushacay.com

Our recommendation
Hire the entire island from $32,250 per night
Enjoy Highview, the 10,000 square-foot, two-bedroom main house, The Landings for in-house entertainment facilities and the Pier House a 3,200 square-foot, two-bedroom beach house on the doorstep of the sea

Best time to visit	**Open all year** **The trade winds that blow through the Bahamas give the islands a warm climate all year round**
Design style	**South Pacific with international accents**
Architects and designers	**Copperfield Bay Team**

In homage to La Belle Epoque, Ara Starck's ceiling-hung canvas in the new Dalí restaurant recalls figures painted by Leon-Maxime Faivre and Theophile Poilpot.

Le Meurice

Paris, France

A chic oasis of calm in the heart of Paris

Host to international royalty and the great fashion designers, Le Meurice is the place where history and the latest design trends meet, a 19th-century architectural 'grand dame' of hospitality with new contemporary and surrealistic twists inspired by Salvador Dalí.

This Muletas lamp is directly inspired by an original drawing by Dalí.

www.lemeurice.com

Our recommendation
La Belle Étoile suite from $24,000 per night
Suite with view of the Tuileries gardens from $5,000 per night

Best time to visit	**All year** **Spring and autumn are particularly special seasons to visit Paris**
Design style	**Charles X and the early 19th century infuse La Belle Étoile Suite, while a contemporary twist on Dalí can be seen downstairs in the reception and other welcome areas**
Architects and designers	**All public areas have been restyled by Philippe Starck and his daughter Ara Starck**
Affiliation	**Dorchester Collection**

In the public areas, various elements reveal the creative flair of the Starcks: the pictorial canvas on the ceiling, signature swan armchairs and homage to the Ancient Greeks.

The Belle Étoile Suite affords a spectacular bird's eye view of Paris from its spacious terrace.

Only steps away from the Louvre, Place de la Concorde and the prestigious boutiques of rue St Honoré and Place Vendôme, Le Meurice boasts one of the most expensive Parisian hotel rooms, La Belle Étoile Suite, decorated in a Charles X style with heavy, opulent drapery, intricate wood panelling and marquetry in striking patterns, complemented by antique chandeliers and murals. The suite is reached by a private elevator that opens directly on to the marble entrance hall and gallery.

The ultraluxe experience here is the spectacular private terrace offering a bird's eye view of the city of Paris, the Seine, Notre Dame and the Louvre. The master bedroom features an impressive king-sized bed and from the windows a view of the Opéra Garnier and Sacré-Coeur. A marble bathroom hosts a gorgeous deep, circular Jacuzzi from which to enjoy the views while the reflective glass throughout the bathroom ensures complete privacy.

Complementing this 'suite experience', downstairs a revolution has occurred with Philippe Starck and his daughter Ara transforming this 19th century 'grand dame' by lifting its Grand Siècle decor of precious interiors and gilded panelling into the 21st century, through the graceful manipulation of colour and light, and by presenting a new interpretation of furniture and a play on transparency and movement. The historic decor is dressed with subtle surrealist touches in homage to one of Le Meurice's more colourful guests,

Salvador Dalí, who resided at the hotel for one month a year for over 30 years. Starck has used Dalí's surrealist work as inspiration and adorned the reception and other welcome areas with contemporary interpretations from sketches that Dalí made of furniture and furnishings – rich satin curtains embroidered with silver thread, a Baccarat crystal iceberg in the centre of the dining room, delicate winged chairs in beech, covered in silver leaf, and three legged tables with feet in the shape of shoes.

Ara Starck has incorporated a hand-painted, 145 square metre, ceiling-hung canvas under Le Dalí restaurant's glass dome in the tradition of Chagall and Cocteau. The images depict four theatrical acts moving through a sublime world in ochre, gold and white. The ultraluxe experience continues at Bar 228 where patrons can order a Croque Meurice and a glass of Dom Perignon. Or perhaps a glass of the very rare Armagnac Darrose 1900 or a Tarragone Millésimée, the liquor of the Chartreux monks.

Restaurant le Meurice with its three Michelin stars offers gracious, elegant dining based on the creative, light and exquisitely flavoured dishes from Yannick Alléno who has artfully presented both the 'Sans', referring to fat-free dishes which includes a sugar-free chocolate mousse, and '100%', which is beside the description of langoustine ravioli with thyme butter.

To support all this indulgence, Spa Valmont, located on the mezzanine, is a haven of peace in marble, wood, stone and glass. Valmont offers a unique range of anti-aging treatments as well as relaxing massages and restorative treatments utilising Thermes Marins de Saint-Malo products, and 'By Terry' for beauty and make up.

The opulent Presidential Suite boasts a private Pompeian-style swimming pool where dolphin mosaics, muralled ceilings and marble tiles evoke Ancient Rome.

Presidential Suite

Hotel Principe di Savoia, Milan, Italy

Roman Empire marries contemporary classics

With its neo-classical facade enclosing a world of service, comfort and luxury, Hotel Principe di Savoia exemplifies the ultraluxe experience. Opt for the Presidential Suite where, after a long day hitting designer boutiques, you can indulge your senses in your very own private Pompeian pool.

Only step into the private elevator and be effortlessly whisked up to the glorious Presidential Suite where, after a brief and very efficient check in, your butler and your personal staff will take care of everything for you.

Even the well seasoned luxury traveller cannot fail to be impressed: here are all the customary elements of a signature grand hotel, from the bespoke linen and cutlery, the deep and luxurious Aubusson-style carpets, to the handcrafted sofas and the mahogany boiserie. The three bedrooms are elegant, in an opulent, traditional fashion, the view from their terrace a delight. But the real attraction is the wet area. Guests who enter here will be astonished by the sheer scale of the Pompeian private swimming pool – it is truly immense. Swim or float at leisure, in the decadent atmosphere of ancient Rome skilfully recreated by the murals, marble tiles and dolphin mosaics. To complete the experience, massage and spa treatments can be enjoyed at the poolside.

www.hotelprincipedisavoia.com

Our recommendation
Presidential Suite from $23,000 per night
Deluxe Mosaic Room from $1500.00 per night

Best time to visit	**All year** **Milan is rich in history, culture, fashion and art and it is the business and design capital of Italy**
Design style	**Unique combination of elegance and classical refinement with state of the art technology and contemporary flourishes**
Architects and designers	**Michael Stelea, HDC Interior Architecture and Design**
Affiliation	**Dorchester Collection**

Singita Grumeti Reserves

Tanzania

"Out of Africa" style luxury in a sustainable conservation environment

With around 350,000 acres of private reserve, this concession area buffering the famous Serengeti in Northern Tanzania is an impressive sustainable tourism initiative committed to the support of local communities and to wildlife conservation. The addition of three exceptionally appointed colonial lodges and a personal guide for the duration of the stay make this a must destination for the true luxury safari lover with a conscience.

Sasakwa Lodge overlooks the Serengeti and is designed in the style of an East Africa manor house.

www.singita.com

Our recommendation
No. 7, The Owner's Cottage at Sasakwa from $15,000 per night

Best time to visit	**All year. The Great Migration occurs between June-August** **Two wet seasons fall between February–May, and October–December, excellent for game viewing. March is traditionally the warmest month with coolest periods being July and August**
Design style	**Each of the three lodges offers an inimitable style. Sasakwa Lodge is perched on a dramatic hill overlooking the Serengeti, designed in the style of an East African ranch house. Set on the grand plains, Sabora Camp harks back to campaign days, with pure 1920s atmosphere. Faru Faru Lodge is a classic East African Safari camp with Zanzibari-Arab influences, located in a discreet riverine valley near the Grumeti River**
Architects and designers	**Wimberly Allison Tong & Goo (WATG)**
Affiliation	**Singita**

Sabora Tented Camp evokes an 'Out of Africa' atmosphere thanks to its colonial style furniture and ethnic artefacts.

Overlooking the Serengeti Plains, Sasakwa Lodge is a hilltop accommodation designed in the style of an East African manor house. It affords panoramic views overlooking the magnificent Serengeti Plains and provides constant game viewing opportunities from the strategically placed Swarovski telescopes.

The experience

Imagine for a moment that you are relaxing on a deck chair in the gardens of Sasakwa. On the plains below, the spectacular migration unfolds, and you reach for the binoculars but realise that the true magic of the moment is to be caught by just absorbing the sheer expanse of your vision. This is the true feeling of being at Sasakwa.

The lodge has six luxurious cottages of between one to three bedrooms, as well as Cottage No. 7, which has four bedrooms and a basement nanny flat. Each cottage has a heated infinity plunge pool and private garden, and bathrooms are stocked with Penhaligon's Quercus range.

The lodge interiors evoke the atmosphere of an elegant colonial club, nostalgically Old-World and adorned with Venetian mirrors, cut glass decanters and crystal chandeliers, in a colour scheme inspired by nature and the bush. There are an extensive library and bar, excellent dining facilities and award winning wines to choose from and enjoy. There is a spa, all weather and clay tennis courts, and a state of the art equestrian centre.

Faru Faru Lodge was designed as an opportunity to relive the excitement of discovery and the simplicity of traditional safari while incorporating local cultural influences. Located on the Grumeti River, Faru Faru shares the area with plenty of regular wildlife visitors, while the architecture blends with the surroundings and allows guests to feel at one with the environment. Two main swimming pools refresh and revitalise on warm Serengeti days, while the lodge has seven air-conditioned suites each with an outside shower and dramatic sliding picture window affording intimate views over two watering holes. An elevated viewing deck looks over the Grumeti River, ensuring that if you decide to stay in for the day, you can still lean over and watch game from the comfort of your chair. But for something really special, and a bird's eye view of the reserve, take a hot air balloon ride across the Serengeti.

For your eyes only

In a different slant on the old colonial theme, Sabora Tented Camp is a 1920s' style tented encampment which conjures an 'Out of Africa' experience for serious romantics as they watch cheetah hunt the surrounding wide open plains, on a background of jazz filtering from the lounge towards the open. Situated right on the Serengeti Plains, Sabora offers six lavish air-conditioned

On warm Serengeti days guests can revitalise in one of the two pools.

tents, each beautifully appointed with campaign style furniture and ethnic artefacts. Sabora brings alive the romantic dream of days of old, while offering every luxury a guest could wish for. The clay tennis court offers a little light exercise – usually with a small audience of zebra, wildebeest and gazelle, and spa services are available for complete relaxation. After a candle-lit dinner punctuated by the occasional distant sounds of nocturnal wildlife, the equatorial night sky invites a stargazing safari.

Professionally guided game drives and walks are a daily feature of life on safari and, for the less active, the spas located at each lodge use Dermalogica products across a range of skin care, facials, massage and relaxation, spa body therapy and hand and foot care. While you lie back and enjoy some super pampering, don't forget to take in the unforgettable views of the Serengeti!

Luxurious and romantic settings for a safari break with all comforts.

Burj Al Arab

Dubai, United Arab Emirates

Billowing Arabian dhow sail and the very essence of Dubai inside

Designed in the shape of a sail, the all-suite Burj Al Arab is an Arab icon, a world of extremes offering one of the finest ultraluxe experiences in the world.

This unique and ground-breaking structure is designed in the shape of a billowing Arabian dhow sail and stands proudly on a man-made island linked to the mainland by a slender causeway. The helipad is located on the 28th floor. At the entrance, four towers propel large fireballs 8 metres into the air in unison with the spray of the giant 20,000-litre Ellipse fountain.

www.burj-al-arab.com

Our recommendation
The Royal Suite from $15,000 per night
A Deluxe Suite from $2,300 per night

Best time to visit	**Between November and April**
Design style	**Architecturally innovative with interiors inspired by Dubai reflecting ancient and revered traditions of Arabian hospitality**
Architects and designers	**Tom Wright WS Atkins Architects and Khuan Chew, KCA International, Interiors**
Affiliation	**Jumeirah Group**

The vibrant colour palette in the lobby and communal areas is inspired by the elements: earth, air, fire, water. Approximately 1,600 square metres of 24-carat gold leaf has been used as embellishment. Beneath the lobby is the Al Mahara restaurant, which can be reached via a three minute simulated submarine voyage. Here guests can enjoy seafood illuminated by the glow of the aquarium.

The interiors have been inspired by Dubai with a robust and vibrant colour palette derived from the elements; earth, air, fire and water, while with extraordinary opulence approximately 1,600 square metres of 24 carat gold leaf were used to embellish the interior. Burj Al Arab is also host to the world's tallest atrium at over 180 metres in height, suffused with warm natural light and flanked by golden columns with a beautiful central fountain where arches of water dance and burst into the air.

The experience

Guests are treated to a royal arrival with a chauffeur driven Rolls Royce transfer from the airport or to a chartered helicopter. As the door opens the 'Marahaba Welcome' is the epitome of true Arabian hospitality and you arrive to rose water, dates, Bakhoor and authentic Arabian coffee.

Discreet check-in is in your suite and there are private reception desks on each of the 27 double-height storeys to sort out any guest requests or queries. A vast number of 'exclusive butlers' is available for every suite – luggage disappears to reappear unpacked and pressed – every convenience, luxury and a highly personalised service are available to you throughout your stay.

Each suite is full of ultraluxe flourishes starting with the view from wall to ceiling windows with breathtaking vistas of the sea and the Arabian Gulf. For those who need to do business, there are also at least six telephones per suite. Comfort is paramount: a pillow menu with 17 options is available and in the massive bathroom, an extensive collection of Hermès toiletries. There is also a bath menu and your butler will advise whether a refreshing Mint Bath or the Extreme Indulgence, with caviar, champagne and strawberries is 'à la mode' that day.

The palatial interiors of the hotel are a feast for the eye, wherever you are, from communal areas to the bedrooms.

Top, right: The marble and gold staircase leading to the master bedroom in the Royal Suite.

For your eyes only

The two Royal Suites are positively stately and span the entire 25th floor. Here, amid palatial surroundings, is the last word in luxury. A private express elevator opens out on the Arabic *majlis* (reception) which boasts a Carrara marble floor and fine mahogany furniture. Guests can enjoy a private cinema, dining room, lounge and library. A marble and gold staircase leads to the master bedroom and a rotating four-poster canopy bed; adjoining is a marble bathroom with spa bath, walk-in shower, Hermes 24, Faubourg fragrances and body products – everything for your pleasure and enjoyment.

The Sahn Eddar, 'the reception of the house', is located at the base of the atrium and is the perfect meeting place to savour morning coffee or an individual chocolate fountain while planning your day, which could be at the hotel or out in Dubai city centre.

In the hotel, there are eight restaurants and bars to choose from and the Al Mahara, an award-winning seafood restaurant, surrounds a sweeping 360 degree aquarium containing deep-blue salt water and filled with brilliantly coloured marine life – one of the hotels highlights. Another essential experience is a pre-dinner drink in the Skyview Bar on the 27th floor overlooking the Arabian Gulf.

Named after a stone known for its purity and healing properties, the Assawan Spa and Health Club is a richly decorated affair and is exclusive to guests. This unique nature-based luxury spa has separate ladies and gentlemen's facilities and offers complete seclusion for guests seeking relaxing and reviving treatments from highly trained professionals. Enjoy spectacular views from the Jacuzzis, spas and pools and sample a vast range of massage and beauty therapies from world-renowned houses such as La Prairie, ESPA and Aromatherapy Associates.

Tear yourself away from the delights of Burj Al Arab and as an honoured guest enjoy a scenic helicopter tour, a luxury chartered yacht cruise or hire a glamorous sports car to drive for the day. For cultural and shopping excursions, Dubai is a vibrant and glittering city. Allow the butler to book an appointment, take the chauffeured Rolls Royce and go to view the beautiful Jumeirah Mosque – a guided tour is recommended so that the sublime interiors can be explained and enjoyed. Hinki Lane is behind the Great Mosque in Bur Dubai at the end of which is the textile souk where literally thousands upon thousands of pashminas and sari silks are available to buy. For a truly Middle Eastern experience, no excursion would be complete without a visit to the Mall of the Emirates or the Gold Souk.

Named after Assawan stone, known for its purity and healing properties, the Assawan Spa & Health Club is lavishly decorated with references to the bathing pools used in ancient Middle Eastern civilisations.

Banyan Tree Al Areen
Bahrain

The essence of Arabia in a spa experience

Al Areen is the Middle East's largest spa, combining ancient Arabian aromatherapy with Asian healing traditions to provide state-of-the-art treatments in one of the world's most extensive hydrothermal gardens, offering the perfect blend of relaxation, adventure and privacy.

A luxurious oasis hideaway fusing contemporary design with Middle Eastern artistry.

www.banyantree.com

Our recommendation
**The Desert Pool Villa from $880 per night
The Royal Pool Villa (with two ensuite bedrooms) from $1,330 per night**

Best time to visit	**November to March, avoid Ramadan and Eid**
Design style	**Arabian Nights**
Architects and designers	**Architrave Design and Planning**
Affiliation	**Banyan Tree Hotels and Resorts**

Banyan Tree Al Areen is a sanctuary for the relaxation and rejuvenation of mind, body and soul, combining an holistic approach to physical and spiritual wellbeing with the use of aromatic oils, herbs and spices – an exotic blend of romance, serenity and sensuality.

The Kingdom of Bahrain consists of an archipelago of 33 islands with fresh and salt water springs that mingle under the sea – a unique geological phenomenon.

Bahrain has an illustrious heritage as a strategic trading seaport, deriving part of its wealth from pearl trading first and then from oil extraction. The ancient Babylonian 'Epic of Gilgamesh' calls Bahrain the 'Garden of Eden' – a fitting epithet for a magical setting where the guest's every wish is granted.

Inspired by the royal gardens of Arabia, Banyan Tree Al Areen features 22 Presidential Royal Pool Villas and 56 single-bedroom Desert Pool Villas, each with their own private courtyard garden, swimming pool and jet-pool.

The experience
Collected by limousine from the international airport, 45 minutes later guests are met by a vista of ancient forts, museums and the sight of Al Khamis, the oldest mosque in the Gulf. The resort also borders the Al-Areen Wildlife

Sanctuary at Zallaq, home to herds of rare Arabian oryx and many other indigenous wildlife species. And for those with a passion for speed, there is easy access to Bahrain's world renowned International F1 Circuit.

Banyan Tree Al Areen's design blends harmoniously with the sublime surroundings of its desert environment. A warm and courteous greeting awaits and, once inside the gates of their private villa, guests can choose to remain there with everything – even optional 24-hour butler service – on hand until check out.

Each of the Desert Pool Villas has a separate ensuite bedroom, living room, dining and seating areas, all arranged around a private, individually temperature controlled open-air swimming pool. The villas are presented in an interesting mix of contemporary and traditional Middle Eastern designs and are havens of privacy and luxurious comfort.

The Royal Pool Villas reflect the mystery and magic of an Arabian Nights fantasy with Arabian architectural elements. A Royal Pool Villa contains all

Redefining desert opulence, the world's most exclusive all-villa luxury spa resort.

the features of its Desert Pool counterpart, but also includes a second ensuite bedroom, a dining room, kitchen, larger azure pool and private courtyard and garden. The extraordinary bathrooms have rainfall showers (both indoor and secluded outdoor versions) and outsized infinity bathtubs. Discreetly placed dishes of perfumed rose-petals complete the scene.

There are three international restaurants to try where the traditional Bahraini cuisine of dates, fish and rice meets Banyan Tree's Far-Eastern heritage and these melded influences join with Western to present an eclectic array of delicious and sensational dishes. Saffron, a Banyan Tree signature restaurant, is situated in the centre of a body of water and accessed by bridge, creating intimate surroundings in which to enjoy Thai cuisine amid opulent Arabian decor. Vertigo combines a sleek and chic interior with an unparalleled view of the Arabian Gulf and offers a selection of international beverages and light food. Set overlooking the spa and featuring elegant Arabian Iwans, rich timber beams and slate, Tamarind is the epitome of calm, highlighted by a cascading waterfall as centrepiece; it serves a wide choice of seafood and distinctive dishes.

For your eyes only

The ultimate jewel in this crown is Banyan Tree Spa. Each of its four sections caters for men and women separately, from lounges to changing rooms and the times to use the hydrotherapy, public swimming pools, hammam, treatment pavilions and health centre. Nestled within a lush and peaceful garden, Banyan Tree Spa Hydrothermal Garden is a sanctuary of wellness and rejuvenation offering an extensive array of features.

Take your pick among Rain Mist Shower, Storm Shower, Ice Igloo, Fusion Shower, Rhassoul, Foot Spa and Herbal Steam Room before venturing along rain mist corridors towards the outdoor vitality pools, where you can experiment with aqua beds, water jet seats and work-out walls.

The hammam garden is the largest in the world. Crowned by a grand dome, it sits within a water garden with cool fountains and invigorating streams, as well as a waterfall curtain tunnel leading to the Outdoor Fountain Courtyard and relaxation area.

Mnemba Island Lodge

Mnemba Island, Zanzibar

Tropical barefoot paradise in these exotic spice islands

Over 1,200 years ago Arab traders in dhows told tales of islands scented with coconut, cinnamon, cloves and spices. Situated three miles off the northeastern tip of Zanzibar or Zayn Zal Bar, meaning 'fair is the island', Mnemba is an exquisite private island occupied exclusively by staff and their guests and reached via a 20-minute transfer by flat-bottomed boat, which sets the tone for this naturally luxurious 'therapy for the spirit'.

A perfect spot on the white sandy beach to spy the tiny turtles as they scramble their way to the ocean.

http://mnemba-island.com

Our recommendation
Any of the 10 beachside bandas from $2,500 per night high season

Best time to visit	**From July to end March** **For big game fishing: Mid January to mid March**
Design style	**Traditional Zanzibari, with grass matting, weaves and thatched roofs**
Architects and designers	**CC Africa and Chris Browne**
Affiliation	**CC Africa**

Mnemba Island is a true barefoot paradise, with only 10 Zanzibari bandas in the cool of the tropical forest, with direct access to the beach.

The whole island is rich in bird and marine life and Mnemba Island Lodge itself is recognised internationally as committed to the protection and conservation of the natural environment.

So it should come as no surprise that these peaceful, white, pristine beaches are the ideal nesting ground for the local turtles and that in fact one of the most absorbing pastimes here is to spy the tiny hatchlings as they scramble their way back into the ocean.

With only ten Zanzibari *bandas* set in the cooling shade of a tropical forest, all with direct access to the immaculate white sand beach, Mnemba is a true barefoot paradise. Built with indigenous materials – mostly pine branches and woven and thatched palm leaves – the *bandas* are open to the cooling breezes and feature wide shady porches. Be hypnotised by the sound of the waves and enjoy romantic dinners at candlelight.

Waking from deep and restful sleep to the warm and welcoming smells of fresh baked coconut bread, guests can roll out of bed and enjoy an early swim and snorkel from their banda or amble around this 1.5 km circumference island girdled by a tropical Indian Ocean coral reef within a marine conservation area. Other, more active pursuits are also available, such as scuba diving. Mnemba is in fact famed for having some of Africa's most magnificent dive locations where several very unusual species of coral reef fish congregate – among them the exotically named Moorish idol, the giant frogfish and the clown triggerfish. And from a safe spot on and above the water, viewing of humpback whales and dolphin are also local highlights

For a well-earned afternoon siesta sample the built in *barazas* on the veranda or a private beach sala with Zanzibari lounger – the perfect place for snoozing on the beachfront and watching the birdlife. If that isn't peaceful enough, then a range of relaxing massages and therapeutic treatments is also available to provide complete rejuvenation from top to toe.

Line and deep-sea fishing are national pastimes here, and newly caught fish, seafood and other tantalising local produce arrive daily on traditional *ngalawa* outriggers. While lunches are enjoyed al fresco, often brought to guests on carved Zanzibar platters, romantic dinners are usually served on the beach, weather permitting, to give a sense of the passing of time in an island that time seems to have forgotten.

Banyan Tree Madivaru

Maldives

A Crusoe-style island paradise

With its breathtaking coral reefs filled with exotic fish, its sparkling sandy beaches and the beautiful, calm blue lagoon, Banyan Tree Madivaru is the stuff of desert island dreams, the perfect setting for the ultimate escapist experience.

Guests enjoy total privacy and the highest levels of service with Island Hosts available 24/7.

www.banyantree.com

Our recommendation
Any of the luxurious six safari style tents with pools each from $2,000 per night for two; price on application for exclusive use of the whole island with up to 18 people

Best time to visit	**Between November and end April**
Design style	**Natural, contemporary Maldivian style**
Architects and designers	**Architrave Design and Planning**
Affiliation	**Banyan Tree Hotels and Resorts**

Each of the six freestanding Tented Pool Villas comprises three individual tents dedicated to different functions: living, sleeping and bathing. They come with a private pool and in-villa spa services.

Banyan Tree Madivaru is situated in the North Ari Atoll of the Maldives and has been designed to provide the ultimate private retreat at this destination. Guests can hire the island exclusively as a romantic hideaway for two or for friends and family to share in this ultraluxe experience. Each of the six freestanding safari-style tents has its own pool and two outdoors showers.

Each Tented Pool Villa comprises three individual tents decorated in 'desert island decor' with handcrafted wooden furniture and timber flooring under luxurious tent canopies. The three tents are organised as discrete living spaces. The living area views out over the pool and beyond to the beach and out to sea; the sleeping area overlooks a private deck and pool; and, last, is the bath area. It contains free-standing bath and shower, and a pair of spa beds for enjoying in-villa couple spa pampering in your own personal oasis of calm with treatments that include a range of signature Banyan Tree Spa massages and facials.

Each villa has a dedicated 'Island Host' who attends to guests' requests around the clock and can organise in-villa dining options or, for the more adventurous, perhaps a unique dining experience – a romantic dinner for two on a sandbank where the only imprints in the sand are yours; or a dinner onboard the exclusive *Madi* yacht.

The *Madi* is a gullet, a 20-metre traditional twin-mast yacht with eight cabins, offering scheduled excursions for guests. Your private marine adventure can start with a fishing expedition in the morning to be followed by sailing the ocean and island-hopping. Enjoy snorkelling or scuba diving with an experienced Banyan Tree dive expert at any number of world-renowned dive sites in the Maldives. For those interested in marine life, dolphin safari and manta spotting are part and parcel of this adventure. At the end of the day, anchor up in a remote spot and, as the sun sets, savour the peace and tranquillity over a quiet dinner.

Back on the island Boa Keyo is the all-day dining restaurant and bar lounge which complements the in-villa dining options and unique epicurean experiences; it is a wonderful place to shelter from the midday sun, to enjoy a drink on the deck and watch the sea.

The African safari interiors exude a calm and inviting atmosphere.

Timber flooring, rattan and teak furniture are complemented by handcrafted wooden accents and luxurious ceiling canopies.

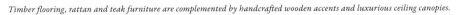

The Oberoi Udaivilās

Udaipur, India

Romance and splendour of a royal era in a city of majestic palaces and lakes

Set against the dramatic backdrop of the Aravalli Hills and steeped in the romance of the historic region of Mewar, The Oberoi Udaivilās is the epitome of what a boutique hotel and luxury resort should be. Situated in the capital of Mewar, Udaipur (the City of Sunrise), within an area of majestic palaces and serene lakes in the heart of Rajasthan, it truly captures the splendour and high romance of a bygone age.

The majestic palace of The Oberoi captures the splendour of a bygone era.

www.udaivilas.com/en-US/Oberoi_Leisure.aspx

Our recommendation
Kohinoor Suite with private pool from $4,150 per night
The Luxury Suites from $3,475
Premier Lake View Rooms with semi-private pool from $895

Best time to visit	**August to end of April**
Design style	**Romantic palatial style set in a bygone era**
Architects and designers	**Parul Jhaveri & Nimish patel with Lim, Teo and Wilkes**
Affiliation	**Oberoi Hotels and Resorts**

At night the gold domes of the palace glow against the deep blue of the sky and the pool.

On a gently undulating hill and spreading down to the banks of Lake Pichola, The Oberoi Udaivilās has been built by local craftsmen in a Mewari style in a glorious natural setting.

This is palatial architecture with courtyards and walks, gently rippling fountains and water features set in exquisitely landscaped gardens replete with sculpture and frescos, arches and domes. The building is further embellished with works of art and craft from in and around the region and commands spectacular views across Lake Pichola of the City Palace and two 17th-century island palaces on the lake, Jag Mandir and Jag Nivas. As night falls, the place becomes almost surreal with the reflection of the pale gold facade of the Oberoi Udaivilās shimmering on the dark waters of one side of the lake and Udaipur reflected on the other – one simply can never have enough beauty.

There are no fewer than nine pools, all the bedrooms are vast, the attention to detail incomparable and staff attend to or anticipate every need.

To dine here is to feast like royalty. The cuisine is international with Suryamahal restaurant providing Thai, Mediterranean and Western choices alongside Udaimahal's traditional and delicious Rajasthani speciality north Indian fare.

The experience

Local activities include visits to The Conservatory, 20 acres run with the permission of the Central Zoo Authority of India. Years ago the area was inhabited by panther, tiger, wild boar, deer, chimpanzee and snakes; sadly, it has been gradually over-hunted and some species driven almost to extinction. Today, wild boar, Indian spotted deer and peacock are maintained to avoid straining the area's ecological balance. The city of Udaipur itself is rich in culture and history with lakeside palaces, forts, temples and bustling bazaars. Udaipur is India's most fabled and romantic city and The Oberoi Udaivilās is its perfect complement.

In keeping with the natural beauty of its surroundings, The Oberoi Spa and Wellness Centre is a haven of serenity with its own pool and lake views. Set

The rich interiors of the lobby welcome guests upon arrival. The experienced staff can organise romantic cruises on Lake Pichola or private dining in the Luxury Suites.

on two floors with a circular atrium, the spa is an experience in itself – the garden courtyard has outdoor dining and a spa menu on offer. On the second floor there are eight therapy suites ideally suited for couples and offering a fusion of holistic treatments drawn from the ancient Ayurvedic and Thai traditions and delivered by highly trained therapists. The Oberoi Spa recipes use only natural ingredients which, of course, are the finest available. For the ultimate pampering experience try the Royal Treasures: sandalwood and turmeric scrubs are applied first, to leave your skin refined and ready to absorb the nourishment of a soothing Tomato Wrap which can also cleanse and tighten the skin. An Oberoi Massage will ease the tension from the body while a fragrant Milk and Rose Bath brings the rejuvenating experience to its perfect end.

For your eyes only
The Premier Lake View Rooms are a unique feature of the resort. All have king-sized bed and private terrace and semi-private pool with a view of Lake Pichola and the gardens. Each of the luxury suites, Great Mogul, Orloff and Regent are exquisitely decorated and each has its own private infinity

swimming pool, steam room and a tented dining pavilion. These suites have unparalleled views of the City Palace horizon and out across the lake where firework displays are reflected in all their glory. Each suite has its own private staff and personal butler to offer round the clock attendance.

For the ultimate space, try the elegant Kohinoor Suite with its fountain courtyards and huge private pool and tented dining pavilion on the patio from which to enjoy magnificent views of the City Palace and the Aravalli Hills. As guests walk through the patri work brass door, the chandelier light dances off the *thikri* (mosaics made of mirrors) in welcome. The suite is beautifully appointed with inlaid furniture, fine art, textiles and traditional hand-knotted carpets. The living room has two real fireplaces for those cold snaps and romantic evenings. There are two bedrooms and the master bedroom suite hosts a king-sized bed; the bathroom looks into a private courtyard, complete with a traditional brightly painted Rajasthan fresco of an elephant, and has a freestanding roll top bathtub and separate sauna and steam shower. There is also a well appointed service pantry. Palatial comforts indeed.

Heavens Above

The Royalton

New York, USA

A thoughtful combination of cutting-edge
design and a traditional sense of luxury

Located in the heart of midtown Manhattan, Royalton is a
stone's throw from Broadway's Theatre District, Times Square
and surrounding nightlife and a short stroll from Fifth Avenue's
shopping and flagship stores. This is a glorious re-imagining of
an iconic hotel, which embraces the vibrant energy of
contemporary Manhattan.

*The re-imagined bar, lobby and general areas of the Royalton bring innovative design
to its devoted, culturally aware visitors from around the globe.*

www.royaltonhotel.com

Our recommendation
**Any of the suites from $900 per night or, if unavailable, book a Deluxe room with the 5ft
round shower from $600 per night**

Best time to visit	**All year for Manhattan's theatre, nightlife and shopping**
Design style	**Innovative, contemporary design**
Architects and designers	**Original design: Philippe Starck** **Overall redesign and new suites: Roman and Williams** **Guestroom design: Studio CMP** **Bar 44 and Brasserie 44: John McDonald**
Affiliation	**Morgans Hotel Group**

Bar 44 has replaced the iconic Round Bar and serves light bar and pre-theatre food.

In this corner of the lobby chill area an icy cast-glass vestibule has been combined with soft suede upholstery and hide-covered chairs to create a dark, masculine space.

In the restaurant Brasserie 44 a lighter atmosphere is achieved with rope arches, glass globes and honeyed teak walls.

Step through The Royalton's signature entrance, an imposing set of floor to ceiling mahogany front doors, into Roman and Williams' stunning lobby renovation: this is the ultimate public space.

A crystalline vestibule filled with textured, handcrafted detail and customised furnishings, where the visual and tactile combination of brass, steel, wood, velvet, suede and fur creates a sense of deeply luxurious comfort coloured with a dash of thoughtfully ambitious design. Hand-blown crystal pendants hang over custom-designed seating while vintage objects detail the space with a touch of well-considered nostalgia. The statement piece here is the monumental cast-bronze fireplace.

There are three new Penthouse apartments with terraces, each designed by Roman and Williams, that expand on the theme of the lobby. Each one is different and entirely exclusive with design influences ranging from Africa to Brazil to Scandinavia – an exciting juxtaposition of cultures and ideas.

All the guestrooms at the Royalton have been updated. They are oversized – in itself a luxury in cramped Manhattan – and are light and airy in contemporary neutral colours. Bathrooms have a 5-foot circular Roman bath and rain effect showers and the walls are mirrored tiles – completely over the top and generating a fitting 'Sex and the City' effect. To heighten the luxury, why not enjoy a spa treatment or massage in the privacy of your guest room.

Just inside the lobby entrance, Bar 44 is an intimate and inviting space for a quiet private drink while Brasserie 44 provides a seasonally inspired menu featuring modern American cuisine complemented by an excellent wine cellar stocked with over 3,000 bottles. Both are ideal for a pre-theatre bite and post-theatre drink.

With the lobby Roman and Williams have created a new 'living room' in the city. A massive bronze fireplace, flanked in a textured iron surround, brings vibrant energy and a collision of cultures in its design.

The Setai

Miami, USA

Asian grace in the heart of Miami

A truly remarkable fusion of Occident and Orient, The Setai literally mesmerises guests with its cutting-edge design and decor, a setting entirely matched by the best traditions of hospitality. Located in the Art-Deco oceanfront district of South Beach, the hotel offers a tranquil respite from Miami's Collins Avenue party scene.

The tasteful fusion between Art Deco design and Asian elements contributes to the unique atmosphere of The Setai, elegant, timeless and serene.

www.setai.com

Our recommendation
The Penthouse from $25,000 per night
An ocean front two roomed speciality suite from $2,700
Suite 3701 has an entertainment room and spa included
Studio suites with courtyard view from $750 per night

Best time to visit	**End November to end April**
Design style	**Art Deco influences with Asian touches**
Architects and designers	**Adrian Zecha**
Affiliation	**The Leading Hotels of the World**

The bar stretches from the lobby towards the courtyard. The dark tube lights, aligned as organ pipes, highlight the shimmering counter-top in mother-of-pearl, in striking contrast with intricate latticework panels in Burmese teak.

A haven of unprecedented luxury and service, this eight-storey, thoughtfully re-imagined Art Deco landmark building was originally constructed in the 1930s as the Dempsey Vanderbilt hotel and is famous for its spectacular series of three grand pools surrounded by palm trees. Like a luscious oasis, this breathtaking and yet calm prospect sets the tone for the general ambience of the hotel with its subtle Asian influences and very un-American serenity. Here the tasteful touch of Adrian Zecha fused together a wide range of authentic materials, from bricks, to bronze plating to leather and tropical lumber.

In stunning and dramatic contrast with the existing structure, another building has recently been added to the complex, right on the beach; it is the Tower which, within its 40 curvaceous storeys in aquamarine glass, hosts the privately owned Penthouse and other speciality suites. Its interiors of teak, black granite and fine silk provide the stylish backdrop for authentic jade art, antique pottery and original paintings, while the bathrooms are clad entirely in absolute black granite and feature large tubs for bathing and personal spa treatments.

This sumptious Penthouse occupies 10,000 square feet on the top floor of the Tower and affords panoramic views of the ocean, beach and Miami skyline, which can also be enjoyed from the rooftop infinity pool and Jacuzzi. It has three bedrooms and comes with its own wine cellar and private butler.

The same soothing serenity in a setting of natural beauty is experienced in the spa, which offers a strictly holistic approach to pampering, as if on a quest to find the elixir of life and eternal youth.

Three entirely different dining experiences are available. These range from the elegant Restaurant, which showcases Asian cuisine by a team of oriental master chefs, to the Grill, which serves simple, good food with an extensive wine list in a more relaxed setting. The Pool and Beach Bar is ideal for patrons who prefer to indulge alongside the 90-foot pool, admiring the beauty of their surroundings.

Three pools grace the property, surrounded by discreet dining pods set within
intimate tropical gardens.

Below and above right: The Specialty Suite is an ideal space to linger in, with generous balconies and astounding views of the turquoise waters of South Beach.

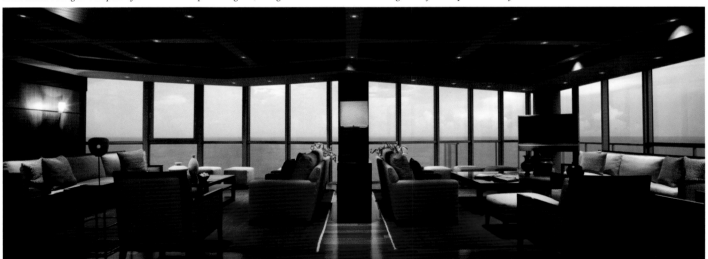

The Hazelton Hotel features a muted, masculine palette of rich browns, dark greens, plums and greys in all the main areas. Ultraluxe touches include a $2 million private screening room with 25 seats.

The Hazelton Hotel

Toronto, Canada

Genuine glamour – a different class of experience

Based in the middle of Yorkville, Toronto's most expensive shopping, clubbing and restaurant district, The Hazelton Hotel delights its guests with its dramatic exterior and interior design, fabulous art and highly attentive designer-dressed staff.

Designed to evoke the ambience and tones of a gentleman's club, the decor of both the hotel's public spaces and its private rooms is a palette of smart dark grey, brown and beige, that blend elegantly with the etched bronze walls and deep grey velvet sofas decorating the lobby.

The building by architects Page + Steele with interiors by Yabu Pushelberg costed around $150 million. This investment has ensured that luxury is palpable in every detail and high quality materials are used throughout. To attract both Hollywood stars and rich business crowds: walls are panelled in cowhide, stone or suede, hallways inlaid with mother-of-pearl and floors covered in green granite.

The hotel guest rooms and private residences have all been given the same VIP treatment. Bedrooms are generously proportioned as are the closets, floor to ceiling mirrors and the eye-catching crocodile-print leather desk chairs. Bathrooms have underfloor heating and are constructed entirely of slabs of dark green granite, with luxurious deep, oversized soaker tubs and separate rain showers.

Ultraluxe touches include a number of exclusive residential suites, private jet concierge and a 25-seat private cinema, ideal for the Toronto International Film Festival and private viewings.

Tempting even the most discerning of palates and attracting guests like Sienna Miller and the Spice Girls, restaurant One provides unpretentious classic North American cuisine, lovingly prepared from wholesome ingredients.

After a day sampling the city's sights, guests can work out in the hotel's fitness centre and unwind in the restful environs of the spa with its four treatment rooms, two steam rooms and elegant mosaic lap pool.

www.thehazeltonhotel.com

Our recommendation
The Bellair Suite from $3,500 per night
A Deluxe Room from $475 per night

Best time to visit	**All year round and a great alternative to New York as a weekend shopping destination**
Design style	**European luxury with North American innovation**
Architects and designers	**Architecture: Page + Steele** **Interiors: Yabu Pushelberg**
Affiliation	**The Leading Small Hotels of the World**

Haymarket Hotel and Townhouse

London, Great Britain

A riot of glorious modern British design

Ideally situated in the heart of London's theatre district, with a magnificent contemporary art collection, the Haymarket is a wonderful interpretation of this landmark Regency building designed by John Nash, a joyous new creation from the vivid imagination of designer Kit Kemp.

Owner and designer Kit Kemp enjoyed combining different and contrasting elements with her customary creative flair. Driftwood accompanies the pastel colours in the soothing conservatory, while a steel sculpture by Tony Cragg is ideally located in the bolder lobby.

www.haymarkethotel.co.uk

Our recommendation
The Townhouse from $6,000 per night
Or a Haymarket Hotel one bedroom suite from $3,500 per night

Best time to visit	All year. There is always something happening in London
Design style	A blend of traditional and modern British design
Architects and designers	Kit Kemp is the co-owner and designer
Affiliation	Firmdale Hotels

The library.

The drawing room of the Townhouse, an exclusive accommodation over four floors with two to five bedrooms.

Dramatic de Goumay wallpaper featuring jungle landscapes covers the walls of the glamorous Shooting Gallery.

Kit Kemp must really have enjoyed creating this small jewel and combining elements as varied as driftwood and chintz textiles, abstract paintings and Persian carpets to ensure that every room represents a real surprise. Contrasting patterns and disparate *objet d'art* that would clash in the hands of a less experienced artist here coexist in a harmonious and joyous design feast, fashioning an atmosphere that lifts the spirit and raises a smile.

All the welcome areas are light and airy with the lobby leading left to the in-house restaurant, Brumus. To the right there are several relaxed spaces: the conservatory is a gentle, art-filled area perfect for tea and reflection; the library provides more pensive surroundings in which to enjoy a quiet drink; and the Shooting Gallery, a glamorous room, is ideal for a private cocktail party or dinner.

The experience

Guestrooms have been decorated individually too and, in a city where space is at a premium, they offer some of the most spacious accommodation. The rooms are characterised by oversised bed heads, an innovative combination of modern and antique furniture married to contemporary chintz and Regency inspired candy-striped cushions in bold colours and interiors that breathe style and comfort at every level. The bathrooms are in granite, oak and glass with walk-in showers and double basins and are stocked with signature Miller Harris toiletries specially created by Kit Kemp for Haymarket Hotel.

The pool is in the basement and for sheer opulence has no equal. It is an arresting electric blue and 60 foot long, flanked by striking gold columns, its water glistening like a rainbow under the light installation. After the exertion, guests can order from a well stocked bar and relax on gold lamé chaises longues. To complete the in-house exercise and pampering amenities, Soholistic looks after body and beauty with a range of treatments and a fully equipped gym and personal trainer on hand.

For your eyes only

The Townhouse has a private entrance with a fully equipped kitchen and dining room for those who wish to use London as a base, but prefer the ambience of a private apartment. Staff and a personal butler are available to cook, clean and help organise activities. The Townhouse can be arranged into a number of bedrooms – from two for an intimate event, to five to accommodate family and friends. It is a home from home and a brilliant idea for those who are seriously 'doing London'.

The sleek swimming pool edged in stone and flanked by opulent gold columns, with pewter bar and spectacular lighting installation by Martin Richman, can be hired for private events.

Marqués de Riscal
A Luxury Collection Hotel, Elciego, Spain

State of the art in design, technology and hotel

In the medieval village of Elciego (Rioja Alavesa), the vineyards of the Marqués de Riscal gave birth to this stunning hotel, a highly innovative combination of cutting-edge architecture and famous winery, perfectly complemented by Vinothérapie by Caudalíe, gourmet dining and, of course, sensational wine.

Glass viewing towers framed in wood emerge among the waves of stainless steel and titatium wrapping the sandstone core of the hotel.

www.luxurycollection.com/marquesderiscal

Our recommendation
The Frank Gehry Suite with private terrace from $1,000 per night
Grand Deluxe Bedroom from $550 per night

Best time to visit	All year, but May to end July especially and around the time of the harvest from September to end November
Design style	**Frank Gehry signature**
Architects and designers	**Frank Gehry architecture and interior design**
Affiliation	**Starwood Hotels & Resorts / The Luxury Collection**

The Gehry Wing houses 14 guest rooms and is linked to the spa and the other 29 rooms by a glass walkway.

The Marqués de Riscal is high comfort in avant-garde design from the hand of Frank Gehry, who has transformed this winery into a two-wing hotel, spa and wine estate experience.

His waves of titanium ribbon-sheeting in pink, gold and silver (signature colours for Marqués de Riscal wine), are wrapped around a sandstone core housing Gehry's interior-designed welcome spaces and 14 guest rooms. Exotic wood, vast beds and spacious bathrooms provide a sense of luxury. The enormous Gehry Suite comes complete with private terrace and breathtaking views across the Sierra de Cantabria. The spa and 29 other guest rooms are situated separately in a second building reached by a glass walkway.

Michelin Starred chef Francis Paniego is the consultant for all the restaurants at Marqués de Riscal and presents modern Spanish cuisine with classic Riojan cooking learned from his mother. There is also a roof top private lounge, and delightful winebar La Vinoteca, where guests can sample creative tapas and wines from across the world (with many Riojas). Wine lovers can tour the Marqués de Riscal winery to view the vineyards and learn about production or enjoy the effects of this local produce at the spa.

Even the pampering has a wine theme, with 15 spa rooms specialising in Caudalíe Vinothérapie Spa treatments providing a wide variety of 'wine therapy' massages and treatments focused on relaxing or energising and anti-aging. All products are made of grape extract and mineral water, packed full of skin-saving properties called polyphenols, and are used to create an exclusive Caudalíe Vinothérapie range of beauty products. Indulge yourself in a Crushed Cabernet and Friction Merlot (scrub and massage) or splash around in a Wine Barrel bath. Not to be missed are the black granite indoor swimming pool, steam room, fitness centre, Jacuzzi and invigorating shower.

Ultraluxe touches at the Marqués de Riscal include personalised check-in and even a pet pillow as well as feeding dishes for your dog, if you have brought your loyal companion with you. Guests are offered a pillow menu with 10 types to choose from to ensure the best sleep possible. And to make your days as pleasurable as the nights, the concierge team is happy to provide information on local places of interest, so guests experience the region's scenery, culture and gastronomy. Let them organise a trip by hot air balloon, horse trekking or, for the really fit, mountain bikes for off-road vineyard adventures, then come back to rest and raise a glass or two.

A Basque Rioja menu can be enjoyed at the gastronomic restaurant, prepared under the supervision of local chef Francis Paniego.

From left to right: the Gehry Wing viewed from the spa , the large pool with relaxing area, and a Grand Deluxe Bedroom.

From its privileged position, the hotel overlooks the medieval village of Elciego, in the heart of the Rioja region.

Town House Galleria is located right above Prada in one of the most exclusive shopping parades in the world, Galleria Vittorio Emanuele II.

Town House Galleria

Milan, Italy

Service Italian style – let your butler fulfil all your dreams

Located on the second and third floors of Galleria Vittorio Emanuele, perhaps the most exclusive shopping arcade on earth, and yet so discreet and understated that you could miss it, Town House Galleria is the first European 'certified' 7 star hotel.

The lighting in each room has been carefully studied by architect Mochetti.

www.townhousegalleria.it

Our recommendation
**The Ambassador Wing from $23,000 per night
or the Verdi Suite from $14,000 per night**

Best time to visit	**All year – except avoid the humidity in August**
Design style	**Tasteful blend of contemporary and traditional styles topped off with state-of-the-art technology**
Architects and designers	**Original arcade: Giuseppe Mengoni (1876)** **Hotel interiors: Ettore Mochetti, with renovations overseen by the Italian Institute of Arts**
Affiliation	**The Leading Small Hotels of the World**

Contemporary furniture and velvet curtains add vibrant dashes of colour to the bedrooms, on a background of coffee and taupe tones.

A chauffeur-driven Bentley will drop you at the red carpet leading to an external private elevator that glides up to the intimate reception on the first floor and a welcome by the team and your butler, who will be responsible for ensuring that your every request is fulfilled.

Architect Mochetti, who is also editor in chief of the Italian *Architectural Digest*, intended the interiors to be modern urban chic, international in their appeal and yet distinctively Milanese in style. In the communal areas he added exclusive individual pieces like a Biedermeier mirror, an 18th-century Chinese console, custom Sawaya & Moroni sofas and slept in every single room to ensure it provided what is expected from the first 7 star hotel in Europe. Given the historical premises, all renovation and decoration work has been carefully supervised by the Italian Institute of Arts and now reveals delightful architectural touches and original frescos.

Despite the grandeur of the Galleria, nothing here is palatial in scale, rather it is cosy, elegant, understated, like a true home from home. There isn't a spa or a swimming pool on site, but a quick trip in the Bentley can solve that.

Location, location, location and superlative concierge services are the real ultraluxe elements of this experience. Each of the 24 double height suites opens on to the Galleria, showing off the divine panorama of cupolas above and providing a bird's eye view of the elegant Prada shoppers below. Named after La Scala's stellar roster of composers – among them Verdi, Toscanini and Bellini – they also come with a private butler on call 24 hours a day to attend to guests' wishes. Elusive tickets to a sold out performance at La Scala, admittance to the most exclusive catwalk and last minute, fast track entry to Leonardo's *Last Supper* can all be arranged with no apparent effort, together with fine jewellery hire and hand made shoe fittings...

Michelin starred chef Giacomo can organise your own private dinner in your room or cater for you and your guests in the signature restaurant Sinfonia, reserved for residents only. The menu, based on Ayurvedic principles and intended to offer balanced nourishment for mind and body, can be fine tuned to fit your personality.

All rooms are double height: a staircase leads to the upper level, where guests will find a work out area, a lounge or a study.

The original parquet floors have been carefully restored and maintained throughout.

Mandarin Oriental

Prague, Czech Republic

Ancient and modern meet in this 14th-century monastery

The Mandarin's trademark standard of service merges with the Gothic and Baroque architecture in a stunning re-imagining of an ancient monastery in the very heart of Prague, with its romantic backdrop of red roofs, turrets and steeples and full view of the medieval castle.

Ancient and modern meet: the hotel occupies the site of a 14th-century monastery, the remains of a Gothic church still visible through the glass floor of the spa.

www.mandarinoriental.com/Prague

Our recommendation
The Penthouse Suite from $6,370 per night
The Mandarin Deluxe Suite from $2,230 per night

Best time to visit	**Late spring and early summer – then September. For 'mushroom safaris' Summer to end Autumn**
Design style	**Modernised Gothic monastery with Baroque and Renaissance features and classic interiors**
Architects and designers	**Architecture: Dům a město architects** **Interiors: Rooms: KCA Interiors; Public areas: Sporer Plus; Spa: Deckelmann Wellness**
Affiliation	**Mandarin Oriental Hotel Group**

The original vaulted ceilings in the lounge invite guest to relax and contemplate.

The vibrant blue bars adds a contemporary twist to the subdued surroundings.

The spa is located in a Renassaince chapel and decorated with thoughtful touches.

In the old quarter of Malá Strana the stone gates and courtyard of a former 14th century Dominican monastery now provide the glorious setting for the three buildings of the Mandarin Oriental.

The hotel's historical features of vaulted ceilings and parquet flooring, Baroque colonnades and arched windows are today complemented by natural materials, vibrant woven rugs, contemporary furniture and subtle Asian touches.

Situated in a private tower at the corner of the monastery building, the Penthouse Suite is a luxurious intimate residence ideal for entertaining, enchanting its guests with breathtaking views of the city's red roofs, its famous castle, the illuminated spires and Petrin Hill. Up to eight guests can enjoy the Baroque splendour of the dining room or a summer al fresco party on the terrace and marvel at how this expansive suite is fitted with the highest specification technology.

In the Mandarin Deluxe Suite high windows let shafts of light spill over the fine oriental silks and parquet flooring, highlighting the interior's rich details, a fitting space for guests to recline in Mandarin Oriental luxury and absorb the monastery's history with views of Prague Castle and the Malá Strana district.

Special places in the hotel include the holistic spa, developed over two floors on the site of a small Renaissance chapel, with glass floor through which to view the carefully preserved ancient ruins of a Gothic church. The Essensia Restaurant and its Baroque dining room offer Asian and modern European cuisine in a series of small, low-lit dining rooms. After dinner guests can retire to the Barego, an extremely chic bar famous for its supreme Martinis, or rest in deep and comfy armchairs under the vaulted ceilings in the Monastery Lounge, whispering secrets over tea and cake after a hard day sight-seeing.

The hotel concierge can provide an insider's city tour to ensure you get the best views of the Vltava River, the eye-catching heights of the ancient castle and cathedral and an escort through the warren of narrow medieval streets and Baroque palaces.

The concierge can also organise tennis coaching at Stvanice, the oldest and most prestigious tennis club in the Czech Republic, where Martina Navratilova, Ivan Lendl and current sensation Nicole Vaidisova played.

And, for a completely different experience, have the concierge arrange a local guide to take you on a mushroom safari to hunt Porcini, chanterelle and Portobello mushrooms that the chef will then cook into a series of tasty dishes.

New York Palace

Budapest, Hungary

The most beautiful café in the world

With its bountiful supply of mineral rich underground water, Budapest is known not only as 'the Paris of the East', but is also one of the world's great spa cities. Conjuring up the grace and romanticism of a bygone era, Budapest's New York Palace is an inspiring blend of magnificence and comfort offering every modern facility in a truly imposing setting.

The exterior architecture of New York Palace pays tribute to the Italian Renaissance style predominant in Hungary at the end of the 19th century.

www.boscolohotels.com/eng/hotels/new_york_palace/5star_hotel_budapest.htm

Our recommendation
The Presidential Suite from $3,973 per night
A Deluxe Room from $1,000 per night

Best time to visit	**All year; spring and autumn are highlights**
Design style	**The hotel is Italian Renaissance and Baroque inspired; the Spa draws on a more contemporary dream of an Alpine ice tunnel**
Architects and designers	**The original building, dating back to 1894, has been refurbished by Boscolo Hotel Engineering and designers Maurizio Papiri and Ádám Tihanyi** **The spa is by Simone Micheli. Lighting in the spa areas and in the lobby is by Nord Light**
Affiliation	**Boscolo Luxury Hotels**

The original and legendary café holds a place of honour in the hotel, while the new areas are designed with contemporary sleek lines and colours.

Built as testimony to the wealth and probity of the New York Insurance Company, the New York Palace and Café opened in 1894. The story goes that Ferenc Molnár, the highly respected playwright and author, and several of his acquaintance were so enchanted by its elegance and ambience that they declared the building must never close – they took the keys and threw them into the Danube to ensure that the café remained open round the clock.

Today, this majestic property has been lovingly restored and refurbished to its 'palace' status by the Boscolo group who uncovered ceiling frescos and works of art hidden or lost in storage that belonged to the original Italian Renaissance and Baroque interiors of marble, bronze, silk and velvet. The original ceiling has been restored, and the glorious panel paintings by Gusztáv Mannheimer and Ferenc Eisenhut depicting cherubs playing, and love and the arts as a reflection of the activity below, are a sight to behold while guests will have their breath taken away by the fountain at the entrance and the Venetian chandeliers that illuminate the arches of the entrance lobby, café and restaurant.

On arrival at the cavernous reception area, check-in occurs around a glass table with a dedicated member of staff to ensure that all the notes on guests are up-to-date and that any special requests or suggestions can be fulfilled.

All the guestrooms are spacious and decorated in muted browns and beige with deep plush carpets, ornate mirrors and Italian furniture. The Presidential Suite is a gorgeous symphony in blue and gold, with exquisite hand-woven silk wallpaper, Murano glass chandeliers and a king-sized bed. The colour scheme complements the eclectic and classical furnishings. The bathroom is wall-to-wall Italian marble with brilliant mosaics and has a deep corner bathtub to bathe in and a separate shower.

The spa and wellness centre at the New York Palace is a fabulous venue: located in the depths, it is a contemporary grotto evocative of an ice cave. Minimalist interiors and subtle lighting conceal a fully equipped gym, mosaic-tiled steam room and a good-sized pool for laps.

A sightseeing cruise on the Danube is a must, especially in the evening when great bridges and historic landmarks such as the Parliament building (modelled on Westminster) are lit up and look their best from the river. Alternatively, take a stroll in the park on Margaret Island, in the middle of the Danube, reached by boat and by bridges at each end – its wooded walks, monastic ruins and ornamental gardens are a delight.

Alpine ice tunnels and Swarovski crystal prisms transport the guests to another world in the spa designed by Italian architect Simone Micheli, with lighting by Nord Light.

Chic elegance is not just reserved for the cream of Russian society. All guests here can delight in the Citterio interiors, enjoy a bio-light detox menu on the terrace and be pampered at the world class Henri Chenot Spa.

Barvikha Hotel & Spa

Moscow, Russia

A perfect combination of elegance, chic and easiness

Barvikha Luxury Village is a new township of high end boutiques in an elegant and green suburb a few miles west of Moscow where most of the wealthy Russian elite have recently taken up residence. This quiet, nearly monastic setting is the new Mecca for the serious spenders, selling everything from Gucci handbags to Lamborghinis, from Harley-Davidsons to the most precious Tiffany jewels...

Barvikha Hotel, the new creation by Antonio Citterio, renowned father of the Bulgari hotels in Milan and Bali, is about to open its doors in the heart of the Village. Here Citterio has taken on a triple role, as architect, interior designer and furniture designer, to ensure that the aristocratic atmosphere of the hotel is carried through in the overall structure just as it is in the smallest detail. The dominant colour palette blends caviar-black and wild rice with strong coffees and chocolates, producing evocative, dramatic and serene interiors. High ceilings, wooden beams in oak and beechwood, marble and grey stone throughout add to the understated elegance of the place. These blend merging it with natural flair to the eco-tech architecture of the exclusive shopping mall located on its doorstep.

Open fireplaces, under-floor heated terraces, extra large bathrooms with steam showers and private spa facilities are scattered throughout the hotel, to break the chastity of the interiors and guarantee individual touches to the seriously spacious bedrooms.

There are two very different restaurants to choose from. The first, nestled in the central courtyard and offering inside or outside dining, falls under the spell of Russian victualler Anatoly Komm, famous for serving traditional Russian cuisine with a contemporary twist. The second restaurant is run under the experienced eye of David Desseaux, who prefers a more international fare, occasionally combined with a bio-light detox menu based on fruit and vegetables for more health-conscious patrons.

Guests tired of shopping can relax in the 2,000 square metre Henri Chenot Spa, a tranquil oasis of 14 therapy suites set to be the jewel in the Barvikha crown. Its exclusive combination of invigoration and rejuvenation therapies for the mind and body embraces ancient Chinese traditions together with modern European techniques and promise a harmonious balance of emotions, well-being and appearance. The large wet area includes an indoor pool for laps and a series of plunge pools, as well as separate saunas and hammam for ladies and gentlemen.

www.barvikhahotel.com

Our recommendation
One of the spa suites from $2,300 per night

Best time to visit	**Early summer and early autumn, for stunning colourful foliage**
Design style	**Modern aristocratic, stoic and masculine**
Architects and designers	**Antonio Citterio; interior lights in the bar area are by Nord Light**
Affiliation	**The Leading Hotels of the World**

Mandarin Oriental

Tokyo, Japan

A sense of space, a sense of place

Mandarin Oriental, Tokyo brings contemporary elegance to Nihonbashi. The perfect blend of oriental refinement and delicacy, of Japan's traditions of physical and spiritual wellbeing with 21st-century levels of comfort – a stay where all the senses are satisfied. Here guests can feast their eyes, pamper both mind and body, delight their palates and savour the special experience that is Japan.

The hotel has been conceived as a single large living tree, where the interiors offer shelter, comfort and gathering areas for the guests, complemented by the signature Mandarin Oriental service.

www.mandarinoriental.com/tokyo

Our recommendation
The Presidential Suite from $9,700
The Oriental Suite from $2,150

Best time to visit	**Spring for blossom and autumn for glorious sunsets**
Design style	**Inspired by 'Woods and Water' reflecting Japan's traditional aesthetic values**
Architects and designers	**Cesar Pelli & Associates Architects and Nihon Sekkei Inc** **Interiors by Lim Teo Wilkes Design Works** **Textiles by Reiko Sudo, Nuno Corporation** **Restaurants, Ryu Kosaka, Nomura Co., Ltd**
Affiliation	**Mandarin Oriental Hotel Group**

In the Mandarin Bar, Judas trees are planted inside transparent boxes that serve as drinking tables.

The hotel is situated in Nihonbashi district, a major mercantile centre during the Edo period of the 1600s, and still a bustling hub.

Its early development is largely credited to the Mitsui family, who based their business there and developed Japan's first department store, Mitsukoshi. Later, Nihonbashi and Edo (Tokyo) emerged as the main financial district, home to the world's second largest stock exchange and as the address where even today centuries-old shops specialise in highly skilled Japanese handicrafts, creating lacquer ware and washi papers and the finest kimono and fans fashioned from silk and bamboo.

In the 21st century, Nihonbashi is the cultural and historical heart of Tokyo, and the Mitsui Property Group and the Mandarin Oriental, Tokyo share a combined 'sense of place' here, within the glorious and dramatic architectural structure of the Nihonbashi Mitsui Tower.

The experience
Conceived as a single, large, living tree with the guestrooms as branches the design is inspired by 'Woods and Water', themes expressed through the use of original materials and evocative motifs on everything from wall treatments, carpets and fabrics to screens and furniture. In keeping with traditional Japanese aesthetics, no single object has been made to stand alone, rather all the elements come together to create harmony. First impressions are everything and having sped up 38 floors by private elevator, you step out into a stunningly chic, glass-enclosed lobby, where all Tokyo appears laid out before you, a breathtaking vista that is revealed from numerous vantage point throughout the hotel as dramatic views of the metropolis including the Imperial Palace Gardens, Tokyo Bay and Mount Fuji, can be enjoyed from the opulent guestrooms and suites, world class restaurants and bar or at the sybaritic spa – a space that has to be seen to be believed.

Accommodation is provided in 179 luxuriously appointed, oversized guest rooms and suites located from the 30th to the 36th floors of the 38-storey Nihonbashi Mitsui Tower and each has a spectacular view of greater Tokyo and beyond.

There are nine dining and entertainment venues including two signature restaurants. At Sense sample modern variations on traditional Cantonese cuisine with chef Kenichi Takase, who prepares authentic and contemporary dishes with great delicacy and flair, producing exquisitely light flavours. For a French-inspired menu, Signature sees an open kitchen with lighter-than-classical, Mediterranean-influenced creations from chef Olivier Rodriguez, who produces sometimes bold, sometimes subtle flavours. For many Japan is synonymous with the tea ceremony and they will not be disappointed. The Sense Tea Corner has more than twenty types of fragrant teas from around the world, from green tea with its powerful healing properties to pu-erh tea

Gently flowing water, subdued lights and monochrome fabrics invite to relaxation in the spa, which affords full views of the city.

for connoisseurs. The elegant Mandarin Bar provides an excellent spot to meet for an aperitif or a smart place to retire after dinner to the sounds of live jazz.

For your eyes only
Something very special, is a rare private wine cellar-in-the-sky, MO Cellar with 5,000 French and other world wines including an eclectic list of organic and bio-dynamic labels – a secret, exclusive to guests at the hotel.

The Spa is an oasis in the city and provides tranquillity, balance and inspiration. Drawing on life-enhancing rituals practised in every culture since the beginning of time, the Spa has combined techniques and philosophies from around the world into a potent blend of treatments that encourage optimal wellbeing. There are nine serene rooms including five suites where guests can be guided through a personal journey of Asian and Western-inspired relaxation, beauty and wellness treatments bringing about the ultimate in spiritual and physical wellbeing. Enjoy the therapeutic effects of the water lounge, jet-bath vitality pool, amethyst crystal steam room and dry sauna; and if you have time, combine these with a 'personalised' treatment such as the signature Time Ritual™ to produce a wonderful sense of purified mind, body and spirit.

Ultraluxe touches include a dedicated staff and a unique 'Isegata' pattern for a Yukata in every room except in the Presidential Suite. Ever since Mitsukoshi

opened a fabric shop here more than 300 years ago, the stories of Nihonbashi and the kimono have been intertwined. The 'Isegata' is mounted on the wall and a collector's item. Master artisans were commissioned to create many original fabrics for these rooms expressing the artistic and cultural traditions of Japan, details that epitomise a rare luxury.

The Japanese appreciation of the singular beauty of individual pieces comes together in an exhilarating harmony in the Presidential Suite.
Here the rooms are vast and the master bedroom has a sizeable walk-in wardrobe. Light floods through the floor to ceiling glass giving a deep sheen to the lengths of walnut flooring. The bathroom is a private spa with a Jacuzzi bathtub right by the glass with stunning views over Tokyo and a choice of water treatments to invigorate or relax. There is a separate study, living and dining room with a table for eight, pantry, hall and powder room for ultraluxe privacy.

An alternative is an Oriental Suite. Here the interiors are reminiscent of forest glades, curtains have a chenille weave in a motif of quercus serrata branches and the bed is covered in a soft, smooth fabric decorated in a tree-leaf theme, conjuring an image of lying down in a bed of fallen leaves of glass. A glass wall stretches the length of the suite with views as far as Mount Fuji or the elegant Imperial Palace and Gardens, which is in walking distance from the hotel. The bathroom is a model of luxury, an irresistible invitation to recline in the spa tub with a view of the busy metropolis over 30 floors below.

Shining Stars
New and exceptional boutique hotels

Orchard Garden Hotel

San Francisco, USA

Innovative design in a sustainable setting

Ideally located within easy walking distance of Chinatown gates, San Francisco's legendary cable cars and the shopping at Union Square, the Orchard Garden is possibly the coolest 'green hotel without being obvious' to be found in any city. With its original artworks, superb restaurant and inviting roof-top garden it admirably succeeds in being environmentally conscious and yet a perfectly credible luxurious boutique hotel.

In green-leaning San Francisco, the Orchard Garden Hotel is innovatively designed to LEED standards without compromising on luxury.

www.theorchardgardenhotel.com

Our recommendation
A Junior Suite with private terrace from $240 per night

Best time to visit	**All year but September and October are the sunniest months**
Design style	**Innovative, modern, spa-like, clean and simple California's first LEED-NC (Leadership in Environmental and Energy Design) certified hotel and the fourth in the world**
Architects and designers	**Architecture International**

111

The private terrace of the Junior Suite is another example of the successful combination of innovative design and sustainable features.

The city of San Francisco is on a mission in terms of green initiatives and the Orchard Garden Hotel ticks all the right boxes in respect of sustainable features and innovative design without sacrificing style, comfort and those little touches of luxury that we expect.

The experience
The sense of calm is immediately palpable from the moment you step into the lobby. The vaulted ceilings, delicate bronze and indigenous floral design elements including a beautiful glass and water sculpture by local artist Archie Held – everything comes together to create an atmosphere of complete serenity which is maintained throughout the hotel.

Roots is a small but stylish restaurant and proudly serves contemporary American cuisine with a Mediterranean flair. The chef is committed to featuring local produce, naturally raised meats and sustainable seafood whenever possible.

Orchard Garden green innovations include everything from the use of reflective roof materials and recycled concrete, steel and paper to chemical-free cleaning products and soy-based inks. Other, simple but effective environmentally friendly solutions that every hotel should put in place include recycling bins in the bedrooms, fresh-air cooling systems and low-flow showers and toilets.

All 86 deluxe bedrooms and suites have a restful, spa-like feel with 100 per cent washable textiles and the use of all-natural bath products. Japanese-style sliding maple doors enhance this soothing effect.

For your eyes only
Head up to the top floor and discover a very rare gem, a delightful rooftop deck bursting with native Californian plants, where you can savour the salt-lick breeze over a glass of chilled wine from the Napa Valley and enjoy the spectacular views across San Francisco and the downtown area.

For the ultimate experience, order a 'NOZONE' from the bar at Roots – a cool-as-a-cucumber experience of Square One Organic Vodka and California-grown European cucumbers, blended with ice and a dash of syrup, then served in a chilled martini glass with a flourish of cucumber as garnish.

All bedrooms feature natural pastel colours, inspiring calm and serenity.

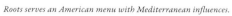

Roots serves an American menu with Mediterranean influences.

Dylan

Dublin, Ireland

Style and experience in a boudoir-chic Victorian townhouse

Convenient for Dublin's vibrant centre, the Dylan is fortunate also to enjoy the peace of its location in the affluent leafy suburb of Ballsbridge, a short walk from the city's historic St Stephen's Green, Grafton Street and Trinity College. Originally designed in 1900 by Albert Edward Murray as the nurses' home for the Royal City of Dublin Hospital, this distinctive Victorian red brick with arches and Dutch gables is now the hottest boutique hotel in town. For its opening in 2007, Dylan added a grey-stone wing, its proportions gracefully echoing those of the older building and connecting the two with glass corridors to create a truly flamboyant experience.

Opposite: The stylish designer library is ideal for intimate meetings.
Below: Dylan Signature suite has custom made furniture by Christopher Guy, like this glorious bed.

www.dylan.ie

Our recommendation
Dylan Signature from $1,200 per night
Dylan Style from $670 per night
Dylan Luxury from $420 per night

Best time to visit	**All year, but spring and autumn in particular**
Design style	**Georgian meets Asian with hints of Rococo**
Architects and designers	**Spirit & Style and HKD**
Affiliation	**Fylan Collection**

At Dylan the emphasis is on individuality, unrivalled personal service and style.
Guests can sip their cocktails at the Spirit & Style large pewter bar and take coffee on the terrace.

The Dylan is a feast for the eyes from the moment one first steps into the chrome-panelled reception area and then into the leather studded lift. The decor is all about arresting colour and sensuous textures with red, midnight blue and white-and-silver walls hung with Baroque mirrors, and interiors offering the comfort of bespoke furniture and the visual pleasure of carefully presented abstract sculptures.

The experience

Once you have taken in the grandeur of the public spaces and admired the impressive library, its tomes all rebound in leather in Dylan's signature colours of green and grey, it is time to move to the real place to be seen – Dylan Bar, highly popular with the in-crowd as well as guests. As you enter your eyes are automatically drawn to the extraordinary Art Nouveau-style pewter bar designed by Spirit & Style, only to be distracted a few seconds later by the opulent button velvet sofas and Murano glass chandeliers on a dramatic lime green and blood red background, and the double sided mirrored fireplace. Take your time to take it all in while you sip what many consider the best Bellini in Dublin or the divine signature 'Dylan' mixed with Stoli and Galliano.

With its pearlised leather dining suites, mirrored bars and individual hanging baby chandeliers for each table, Still is a luxurious and comfortable restaurant in which to enjoy French and modern Irish cuisine. Executive chef Padraic Hayden has put together an imaginative contemporary menu drawing on fresh local produce to create a range of fabulous dishes. Ask for a table by the window to enjoy people watching over lunch and for a cosy corner table in the evening for privacy. As you relax, take the advice of Sommelier Camilla Guidolin, who oversees a selected cellar of more than 230 wines, and be tempted to explore new drinking experiences at her recommendation.

For your eyes only

Indulge in an in-room massage and take your pick from the offerings on the exclusive 'his and hers' bath menu; luxuriate in a candle-lit, rose petal-filled bath and rest assured that your night is well taken care of. At Dylan, they take the quality of guests' sleep very seriously so there is a pillow menu and a memory foam Seventh Heaven bed dressed in the finest Italian Frette linens in which to enjoy the most restorative sleep of your life. You can even purchase the bed there and then!

A baby Guggenheim-style spiral staircase is one of the new features to this restored grade II listed building.

Andaz

London, Great Britain

Personal style in a Big boutique

The Andaz is the benchmark for a number of new hotels around the world that pride themselves on *andaz,* an Urdu word meaning 'personal style' – a style created for guests who want all the luxury of a five star hotel without the formality. The Andaz guest is looking for a fresh, uncomplicated luxury with discreetly personalised service.

The Living Room is an area of calm, featuring art pieces like this wood sculpure by David Nash.

www.london.liverpoolstreet.andaz.com

Our recommendation
Andaz Suite King from $1,164 per night
Andaz Open Plan Suite from $1,408 per night

Best time to visit	**All year**
	The hotel has a loyal base of business clientele during the week, which makes it a delicious haven for art and architecture lovers at weekends
Design style	**Modern classic**
Architects and designers	**Barry Bros, Conran & Partners, John Atkin, Fitch, Wilsdon Design Associates, Global Hyatt Corporation and JER Partners**
Affiliation	**Hyatt Hotels and Resorts**

Opposite: The grand and dramatic interior of Aurora, with its huge stained-glass dome. Above: A side elevation view of the Living Room – with leather chairs by Dema, Mathew Chambers geometric shapes on plinths, sofas by Minotti and the Jack Milroy figure cut outs by the entrance to the lifts.

This beautifully restored Grade II listed building boasts a host of Victorian architectural features which complement imaginatively designed contemporary interiors. Each space showcases contemporary art and photography, reflecting Andaz's position in the hearts of local residents and artists living and working around Liverpool Street, in Hoxton and Spitalfield. It is these locals who provide 'Eastern Thinking' a series of quotations to be found throughout the hotel.

The experience
Since there is no official reception area, a host greets hotel guests in the living room, a congenial space furnished in contemporary style, displaying art works and messages from local residents that are integral to the ambience. Coffees and refreshments are served while the luggage is whisked away and the host notes personal preferences and suggests ways to enhance the visit.

With an array of restaurants to choose from within the hotel, guests can enjoy creating their own menus from the comfort of their room or can put together their own event menu in the Andaz Studio, a private dining space featuring an open kitchen and private bar.

Every taste is catered for at Andaz. The Aurora restaurant offers fine European cuisine with a bar that serves classic cocktails and a connoisseur's wine list. Aurora's most magnificent feature is an original stained-glass dome ceiling in this elegant, brasserie-style setting.

Fresh fish restaurant Catch is where dinners come to enjoy succulent oysters or choose from an imaginative menu either at table or at the attached horseshoe shaped Champagne Bar with its eye-catching silver and blue mosaics.

Each of the 267 rooms, which include 23 suites, has an individually designed interior. Suites on the fifth and sixth floors have a light and airy 'loft' feel while those on the lower floors boast higher ceilings and period features typical of late Victoriana but everywhere the interior design is distinctly modern with the accent on comfort.

Andaz staff can organise an East End Contemporary Art tour with a local artist to escort guests to artists' studios and the more secluded galleries. The hotel is in easy reach of magnificent historical London landmarks such as St Paul's, and arresting contemporary architecture like Norman Foster's Swiss Re Building or Richard Rogers' Lloyds of London. Also within walking distance is Tate Modern as are numerous local markets and shops.

Hôtel Particulier

Paris, France

A bijou hideaway in romantic Montmartre

Secluded within its own private garden sits a treasure trove, a hotel that captures the essence of Paris' artists' quarter and seamlessly fashions it into a truly extraordinary sensory experience.

The Particulier offers an extraordinary sensory experience. For example, the Curtain of Hair room has a special audio system that allows guests to record secrets in a speaker box, for the benefit of the next visitors.

www.hotel-particulier-montmartre.com

Our recommendation
The Curtain of Hair Room from $800 per night

Best time to visit	**Spring**
Design style	**Directoire-style townhouse with contemporary artistic interpretations**
Architects and designers	**Re-imagined by Morgane Rousseau and Fréderic Comtet and with contributions from Mathieu Paillard (Agent M)**
Affiliation	**Hoosta Style Hotels Collection**

Private living room and garden.

The oldest, most original hotel in Montmartre, the 'Mansion in the garden' has played host to many illustrious residents from the arts, from actor Claude Roze, better known as Roze de Rosimond, who replaced Molière and, like the master, died on stage, to Pierre-August Renoir who, as a struggling young artist, worked for the glamorous Hermès family.

With a panoramic view of the Eiffel Tower from its gate, L'Hôtel Particulier de Montmartre is a 'classic secret' in Parisian circles. With a bit of luck and a good map, a short, well hidden paved path nestling between avenue Junot and rue Lepic will lead you to the 'Rocher de sorcière' (the witch's rock) and from there to the hotel gate.

The experience
Through the gate, and suddenly it is as if you have chanced upon another world. Waiting on the other side is the mystical evergreen garden, designed by Louis Benech (the name behind the Tuileries). Imagined as a symphony of plants, it offers a harmonious green palette on which to rest the eyes while enjoying a delicious continental breakfast among the flowers and foliage.

The hotel is a reflection of a rich artistic heritage. Enter, and the serene setting of 'Le petit salon de lecture' welcomes you like an aristocratic reading room of old with its extensive array of *objets d'art*, first editions and reviews. Books on contemporary art, fashion, architecture, music, photography and design bear testimony to the art historical life blood of the mansion.

Beyond the entrance, pause to admire the fine furniture in the private living room, where a first edition Arne Jacobsen 'Egg Chair' and a Barcelona Chair by Mies van der Rohe coexist in perfect harmony thanks to the unerring eye of Mats Haglund, his vision refined by such prestigious commissions as the refurbishment of the Chanel boutique.

Further arresting pieces, antique, Baroque and contemporary and all collected by the present owners, adorn the restaurant while outside on the green terrace the poetically bubbling fountain offers diners a soothing prospect.

Each of the five fabulous suites was created by a different artist, designer, sculptor or architect. Here the bedroom and bathroom of 'Tree with Ears'.

For your eyes only

Upstairs are five luxuriously appointed and delightfully comfortable suites, each with a unique contemporary theme – the inspiration of a different artist, designer or architect.

The 'Curtain of Hair' room by artist and photographer Natacha Lesueur plays on materials and transparencies while the equally innovative 'Trees with Ears' room, designed by illustrator, art director and consultant for Benetton Pierre Fiechefeux, draws on Japanese influences to create a work of 'shapes, lights and shades'.

Inspired by nature, contemporary artist Martine Aballea's 'Chambre Végétale' envelops guests in a 'luminous, soft and flowered space' while Olivier Saillard's 'Poems and Hats' suite is infused with his experience as curator of the Marseilles Fashion Museum.

Finally, painter and Marcel Duchamp prize winning sculptor Philippe Mayaux's glistening 'Vitrine Room' references a fabled Parisian patisserie with glass pieces resembling cakes in glass display cases.

The hotel facade reflects the glory of St Stephen Cathedral, visible from most of the rooms and a key feature of the private dining experience at DO & CO.

www.doco.com/english/index_hotel_eng.htm

Our recommendation
There are two suites from $1,200 per night

Best time to visit	September to end of June are optimal, Vienna is a year-round destination
Design style	Modern luxury with Byzantine touches and Austrian flourishes
Architects and designers	Hans Hollein Architect Colin Finnegan, Gerard Glintmeijer FG Stijl interiors
Affiliation	Design Hotels

DO & CO Hotel

Vienna, Austria

A feast for the senses

Vienna. Fabled for its cultural life, its architecture, its waltz and, above all, for its cooking. Set in this city of Old World charm and modern energy, DO & CO is a hotel for gourmets in one of Europe's gourmet capitals.

In 1981, a small delicatessen and restaurant in the heart of Vienna started serving the most exquisite international fare. So delicious was the food that requests for catering came thick and fast and today the business is global, serving elite private clients and famous brands such as BMW and Formula 1. The DO & CO recipe for success, mouth-watering dishes and beautiful presentation combined with charming and attentive service, were natural ingredients for a DO & CO Hotel in Vienna, created by the addition of luxurious surroundings.

The hotel is located in Vienna's historic District 1, famed for its stately buildings, its museums, its white stallions, mirrored halls, masked balls, music festivals and angelic choirboys performing against the backdrop of lavish concert halls.

DO & CO occupies seven floors, from the third to the top, of what is a Viennese design icon. The glass mirror-walled facade of Hans Haus, an architectural landmark, has been designed for DO & CO by Pritzker prize-winning architect Hans Hollein. Making a permanent visual connection between ancient and modern, the glass facade reflects the glory of the 12th-century St Stephen's Cathedral and its massive Pummerin bell which still announces the New Year.

The experience
DO & CO hotel interiors reflect heritage high quality natural materials such as teak and stone, 'cleverly integrated into a futuristic vision of modern design'. The hotel boasts one of the hippest bars in Austria, an extremely popular restaurant and a stylish selection of guest rooms.

Located on the sixth floor is the Onyx Bar, its panoramic views of the Vienna skyline enjoyed from comfortable lounge chairs and sofas by day, while after dark it turns into Vienna's hottest night spot offering delicate sashimi hors d'oeuvres and signature cocktails plus DO & CO's exemplary wine list. The 'temple' is a private dining pavilion for up to 12 guests with unparalleled views of the city skyline.

The DO & CO Restaurant on the seventh floor has an open kitchen and caters to a wide variety of tastes. Choose from a spice experience at a private wok station, order the finest sushi and sashimi or sample the best kebab rotisserie in Vienna. In a city legendary for its cuisine, there are also traditional Austrian dishes to savour. Theirs is a highly eclectic menu reflecting the hotel's roots as gourmet entertainment – and it's extremely popular.

For your eyes only
Considerate service extends to catering for your plane trip back home – a little hamper of delicious goodies will tantalise your less fortunate flight companions. Let the concierge organise an excursion to the world-renowned Spanish Riding School and watch the famous Lipizzaners.

Split-level guest rooms are shaped like slices of Viennese Sacher torte. Each comes with a box of wickedly divine Demel chocolates – indulge as you relax on the soft kilim bedspreads or lounge in the comfort of the piccalilli-yellow deep suede sofas. Then treat yourself to the Jacuzzi and massive transparent shower in the bathroom.

There are two DO & CO Suites, each with a fully stocked bar and a private terrace that enchants guests with a bird's-eye view of the cathedral. The suites also include a private spa experience with steam bath and Jacuzzi; the concierge team will be happy to organise hairdressing, beauty and make up and massage appointments in the privacy of your suite.

The Gray

Milan, Italy

A private club swathed in the scent of quiet exclusivity

Tucked away between the Duomo and La Scala and a stone's throw from Galleria Vittorio Emanuele in the heart of Milan's financial and shopping district, The Gray is akin to an exclusive club. Once a member, you will never want to stay anywhere else.

Contemporary and playful in character, the interior design by Guido Ciompi is meant to play tricks on the eye with decorative pieces fixed to the walls and this beautiful swinging seat in the centre of the lobby.

www.hotelthegray.com

Our recommendation
Gallery View room from $1,000 per night

Best time to visit	**All year; best to avoid muggy August**
Design style	**Double identity – history and tradition meet exquisite modernity**
Architects and designers	**Guido Ciompi** **Lighting by Nord Light**
Affiliation	**Sina Hotels**

A carefully planned lighting scheme set the tone for elegant dining at Le Noir, situated on the first floor.

The Gray is Milan's quintessential boutique hotel, a benchmark for style and discretion, providing a rarely encountered level of service. Its conception is a flawless reflection of modernity and timelessness in a city famed for its food, fashion, design and architecture. Regular guests know that their foibles are cherished and their requests always graciously met. And they are prepared to pay a premium for this.

Behind the careful refurbishment of these historic premises is Florentine architect Guido Ciompi, of Gucci boutique fame. From the moment you enter the silver-walled lobby you realise that contemporary designer chic dominates the scene. The attention grabbing, shocking pink swing seat hanging in the centre of the silver-walled lobby is deliberately positioned and lit to introduce you to a host of design touches, and is complemented by a series of red velvet sofas and low back brown leather chairs. Throughout the ground floor and lobby carefully recessed and spotlit niches reveal beautiful

designer evening gowns worn by models and celebrities of yesteryear.

Each of the 21 guest rooms is unique – some have four-poster beds suspended from the ceiling, two have a private gym, Turkish bath or Jacuzzi bath. All are enriched with travertine, wooden floors in ebony, brilliant silk coloured covers, plush velvets, crystal, zebra and ostrich skins and other exotic African fabrics.

The experience

The Gray's concierge team don't just know about the downtown scene – they are part of it. From restaurants to nightclubs to the most exclusive stores, latest exhibitions and private views, even last minute tickets to La Scala – they have access to them all. During the day let them arrange a personal shopper to take you around Milan's fashion stores, to be followed by a well earned massage in the privacy of your own room.

At the minimalist G Bar, just off the foyer, house cocktail supremo Pedro Fiol will be pleased to create something unique and original just for you – or mix

Above, below and bottom right: The GBar has conic shaped lamps dressed in white silk with sandblast crystal shelves, red velvet sofas with a shocking pink finish.

Top: The Gallery View Room opens onto a terrace with views of the Galleria Vittorio Emanuele.

you his signature Mojito to enjoy while lounging against the bar's deep, soft red velvet sofas, watching other patrons and local fashionistas come and go. Small tables that light from within, offsetting the dimming of natural daylight, add to the atmosphere.

Then adjourn to Le Noir restaurant, a Post-modern cocooned oasis where a dramatic, black velvet sofa-bench and black and white padded cushions along one side and Kvadrat chairs and small leather armchairs are complemented by a carefully planned lighting scheme. Here chef Luciano Sarzi Sartori reigns, tantalising guests with an ever changing selection of Mediterranean dishes based on traditional Italian recipes and using local and seasonal produce: hand-made pasta, fresh fish and vegetables ... And the wine list, full of majestic Italian greats, boasts a growing number of organic wines.

Alternatively, in the summer months try Aria. Part of Le Noir, Aria is an open-air lounge, virtually a unique space in Milan and perfect for alfresco dining with a few friends. Once again, Sartori will happily preside over the menu and wine list for you.

The facade and the individually designed rooms of the Sixty Hotel reflect the appeal of the fashion brand with young and stylish customers.

Sixty Hotel

Riccione, Italy

Young at heart luxury, fashion style

Sixty Group, a leading name in fashion for the young, has recently teamed up with Boscolo Group to launch a luxury hotel chain to match its pop-fashion image.

The funky new premium hotel in Riccione, the Italian capital of summer entertainment, is the first fruit of the collaboration between the enthusiasm and creativity typical of the fashion brand and the experience provided by the more established hotel, bringing luxury to a new market.

In order to maximise the connection with the retail branch of the group, the hotel occupies a site next to a series of boutiques and shops in overhaul of a typical Fifties seaside hotel has been directed by Studio 63, the name behind all Miss Sixty and Energie boutiques, while the design and furniture of the interiors have been treated to the personal attention of Wichy Hassan.

The eye-catching facade of the hotel is dotted with large, elliptical openings that reveal balconies at a different orientation. At night this ultramodern, playful design is set off by a clever lighting system put in place by Nord Light and the rooftop garden becomes a party scene.

Probably inspired by illustrious predecessors such as Puerta America and Fox Hotel, Sixty's creative director Wichy Hassan chose to personalise each floor and each room in a bold interpretation of the brand. Progressing from street level to the fifth floor, guests are greeted by a range of strong colour themes, from yellow, to green, to orange to black. Back-lit curving pillars of sheet plastic line the walls, with lights illuminating the corridors at a different intensity or flickering at different speed.

Each of the 39 rooms has been styled by a young artist who has simply added two dimensional murals, sometimes venturing over the ceiling, beds and cupboards to complete the effect. The final results range from the fairytale innocence of Vidya Gastaldon's room, to the playful 'Eden of Doodles' by Jon Burgeman to the dark Hitchcock mood created by Nicola Gobbetto, complete with the words 'Someone Was Killed in This Room'.

In such an environment, where living life to the full, shopping and having fun are of the utmost importance, guests are also able to communicate with each other by webcam located in their bedrooms, expanding boundaries in a truly innovative way.

www.sixtyhotel.com

Our recommendation
Book the only Suite by Wichy Hassan, on the third floor from $600

Best time to visit	**July and August, to enjoy the party scene on the beach**
Design style	**Pop-fashion, contemporary, artistic and young**
Architects and designers	**Hotel project: Studio 63** **Interiors and furnishing: Wichy Hassan** **Individual rooms by 30 young artists**
Affiliation	**Design Hotels**

Contemporary interiors and designer furniture contrast with the remains of a 14th-century water tower, discovered during the construction.

Lánchíd 19

Budapest, Hungary

An innovative artwork shaping the new spirit of Budapest

Situated in the shadow of Buda Castle and next to William Tierney Clark's historic Chain Bridge, from which the hotel takes its name, Hungary's first Design Hotel, Lánchíd 19, stands like a contemporary urban lighthouse on the Danube riverbank, its arresting design attracting the attention of passers-by.

In the breeze the glass-panelled facade waves back and forth. A kinetic artwork in the form of a glass curtain that reflects and reacts to the movement of the Danube, it ripples according to the strength of the river flow. Each panel is etched with tiny water-themed imagery depicting minute aquatic motifs and objects that one might find in the river – a diver, a ring – and repeated throughout its owner Csaba Valkó's thumbprint, a whorl, echoing the pattern created when a stone is thrown into water.

There are glass suspension bridges on the storeys leading to the rooms. Highly regarded member of the School of Paris, French artist Françoise Gilot's canvases are celebrated in the reception with three original works, *Break of Day, Firebird* and *Enthusiasm,* while interiors and guest rooms enjoy original artwork commissioned from art students.

The river water imagery is echoed inside with walkways backlit to produce a ripple effect. Guests who want to take in the vista from their river front rooms simply press a button and the glass sheets slide away to reveal stunning views of Margaret Island and the Pest riverbank.

From their vantage point on the seventh and top storey of the hotel, the three aptly named Panorama Suites offer unrivalled views: two face the Pest river while one faces Buda Royal Castle and the city's historic core of medieval, Baroque and 19th-century buildings. Decorated in minimalist style, they feature a chunky glass mosaic which reflects the lights to create a wave-like refraction on the walls. The suites have their own Panorama terrace for private outdoor relaxation and large bathrooms that share the views.

The whole of the first floor is given over to L19, a highly rated restaurant serving both contemporary and traditional Hungarian cuisine. There is also a secret lounge and glass floor situated above the exposed excavations of a 14th-century water tower unearthed during construction.

www.lanchid19hotel.hu

Our recommendation
Three Panorama Suites from $700 per night

Best time to visit	**Spring, summer and autumn**
Design style	**Contemporary and innovative**
Architects and designers	**Szövetség 39 and NextLab**
Affiliation	**Design Hotels**

In the lobby, a clear-beaded curtain snakes its way around long, low curved pink velvet sofas and oval rugs.

The Park

New Delhi, India

Space age urban design destination

Its design inspired by the five primary elements – fire, water, earth, wind and space of the science of Vaastu Shustra – The Park captivates the spirit and stimulates the senses with its colours, textures and form, an architecture conveyed through movement, light and transparency. A totally Indian experience in an entirely luxurious setting.

Just outside the lobby, award winning Fire restaurant offers a unique Indian cuisine experience.

http://newdelhi.theparkhotels.com

Our recommendation
The Residence, two private floors on the 9th and 10th floors. Book either a Deluxe Suite from $750 per night or one of the four Presidential Suites from $1,300 per night

Best time to visit	October to May
Design style	Vaastu Shustra
Architects and designers	Conran and Partners / Apeejay Projects, Apeejan Surrendra Group
Affiliation	Design Hotels

At night the open deck of the Aqua area becomes a stage, with a giant revolving mirror ball projecting over the pool. Timber pavillions, enclosed with white curtains, offer private areas for drinking, dining or massage. Aqua pool side bars are local favourites.

Superbly positioned on Connaught Place in the heart of the capital's business and entertainment area, this delightful boutique hotel is ideally placed for shopping in the city's luxury label stores, for sampling its rich culture and architecture and for surveying its sheer human diversity.

The experience

Enter the hotel's dramatically curved, brilliant white lobby and your eyes are immediately drawn to the artworks and your spirits lifted by a pervasive sense of calm. The space is defined by Paul Cocksedge's *Neon*, clear glass capsules suspended in groups from the ceiling and filled with neon that glow magically in the dark. As if she had The Park in mind, Diana Vreeland, former editor of American *Vogue*, famously wrote: 'Pink is the navy blue of India'. Pink, a theme repeated throughout the hotel as the Indian colour of celebration and the Hindu elemental theme of Vaastu Shustra's 'earth', is also the colour of the two seated sculptures at the entrance and of the oval pink rugs on which sit welcoming pink velvet sofas and armchairs – all custom made by Conran and Partners.

Fire, the contemporary Indian restaurant, is conveniently situated to one side of the lobby, its kitchen under the watchful eye of award winning Executive Chef Bakshish Dean. Let him tempt you with specially created dishes that subtly blend flavours and spices; or try the Chaat platter, a row of delicious Indian street favourites presented sushi-style.

Separated from the restaurant by an eye-level curved bronze wall, the highly popular Agni bar is an exciting, passion-filled space with devilishly wicked touches. The 35-foot bar is the stage where mixologists create classic cocktails and dream up new concoctions such as the Rose Martini and Seasonal Fruit Margarita or offer a Satan's Whiskers cocktail for after sunset enjoyment.

A second restaurant, Mist, introduces the element of water into the hotel's design with blue glass beaded curtains creating random patterns of water droplets along the opaque glass wall. A projected art video or installation will complement the Italian influenced menu.

The Terrace and Aqua Garden are the alfresco experiences by the pool with a live grill and barbeque counters to spice up a chilly winter evening in the capital.

Light blue is the predominant colour, and the circle is the main decorative motif in Mist, the 24 hour restaurant with Italian influences.

The pale watery green walls and dark intimate interiors in rough natural slate at Aura, the spa zone.

On The Terrace daily yoga classes are held for guests to start the day. Spiritually refreshed, why not reinvigorate the body at Aura, The Park's new day spa and achieve a Nirvana like state of complete relaxation and wellbeing. Treatments include traditional Ayurvedic therapies and signature beauty preparations that call for rare combinations of natural herbs, flowers and spices and draw on ancient traditions; inhale the scent of fruit based body wraps and scrubs made from milk, honey, lavender and sweet basil ...

For your eyes only

The Residence has two ultraluxurious private floors where the Deluxe and Presidential Suites are located. Here, the elements of earth and the city of Delhi are the design inspiration – rust and green tones harmonise with slender troughs of live wheat grass. A private lounge with Luyten's inspired furniture and windows offers breathtaking views out onto the 18th-century observatory Jantar Mantar and the lush green gardens of the Capital – the perfect setting to take tea and browse through a newspaper.

These private rooms are extensive, their graceful design embellished with leather furniture, suede bedspreads and green and orange rugs. The bathrooms have huge Japanese-style Satwario marble baths and rain showers and are generously supplied with Ayurvedic toiletries.

The extensive bedrooms in the Presidential Suites feature leather furniture and suede bedspreads in rust and beige colours.

Hôtel de la Paix

Siem Reap, Cambodia

Respecting the past, embracing the future

One of the world's new luxury destinations, this seriously stylish five star boutique property offers outstanding levels of comfort combined with world class dining and spa facilities. Only footsteps away from colourful markets and a vibrant night life, guests can enjoy complete peace as the hotel is set around an inner courtyard with tranquil gardens and water features.

Art Deco inspired design is complemented by strong Khmer influences.

www.hoteldelapaixangkor.com

Our recommendation
Duplex Spa Suite from $450 per night

Best time to visit	**October to March**
Design style	**A hip combination of art deco and traditional Khmer design**
Architects and designers	**Bill Bensley**
Affiliation	**A BMC Management hotel Small Luxury Hotels of the World**

The Fireflame Courtyard Garden.

Siem Reap is the heart of modern Cambodia, a country full of tropical beaches and lush forests. It is also the gateway to Angkor, the Khmer Empire's ancient capital and home to the magnificent 12th century temples of Angkor Wat, Angkor Thom and Bayon.

Hôtel de la Paix is committed to responsible tourism through a number of initiatives that support the local community. Drop in at the hotel's Arts Lounge, a live space dedicated to the celebration of Cambodia's rich cultural heritage, and enjoy an ever-changing exhibition of original works of art and performances in an atmospheric and thought-provoking setting.

The experience
Fine dining is central to the hotel's ethos. Under the leadership of Joannes Riviere, the Executive Chef, the hotel's signature Meric, named after a Cambodian pepper, is proud to support the revival of Khmer cuisine.

Exotic-sounding rice such as Red Cat, Serpent's Neck and Elephant's Tail entices guests to sample authentic recipes made with wild honey, roots and tubers, flowers, herbs and the region's indigenous small fish. And for those seeking a more contemporary and international dishes, Riviere presents a menu that draws on his experience in France and USA, but one still based on fresh local ingredients. An alternative, less formal venue is Café de la Paix, a mouth-watering 'gourmet deli for the global nomad', providing handmade ice cream, frozen yoghurt and Italian gelato, attracting customers from all over town. There are 12 exotic flavours to choose from – try the Madagascan bourbon vanilla ice cream, blueberry-frozen yoghurt or, most popular, the rich sticky chocolate.

As a delicious accompaniment to your excursions have the chef organise an exquisite hamper to enhance your memories – a gourmet's dream with Dom Perignon Champagne, foie gras, salmon and dill coulibiac, lemongrass king prawn salad, wild mushroom salad, tropical fruit and strawberries.

Pampering the body here becomes a spiritual as well as physical experience. Spa Indochine overlooks a Khmer-inspired swimming pool and water

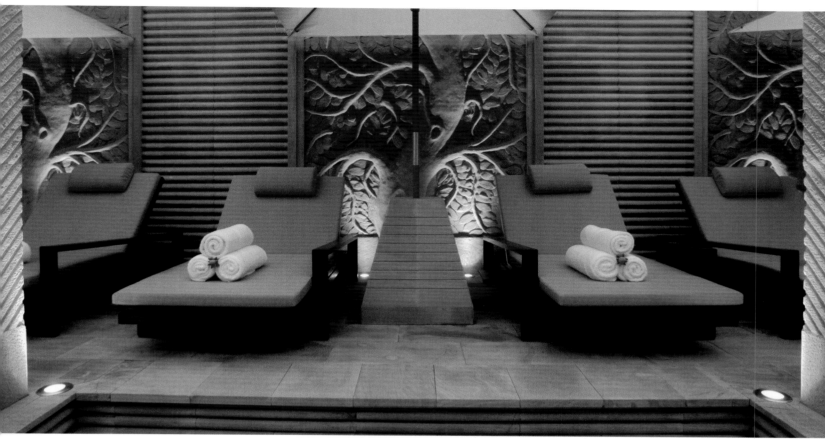

The relaxation area beside the pool at Spa Indochine, a three-storey haven of peace and tranquillity.

Café de la Paix attracts customers from all over town with its selection of frozen yoghurts and ice creams.

garden and is a space devoted to peace and tranquillity. Begin with a foot-cleansing ritual using an essential oil soak while you sip a restorative blend of herbal tea to a background of restful music. Once blissfully relaxed, choose from up to five hours of luxurious treatments in a single sitting and indulge in The Angkor Wat with its flower foot scrub, body scrub then body wrap, followed by an hour's body massage, a facial, an oriental foot massage and an Elixir to purify and invigorate body and soul.

For your eyes only

The Duplex Spa Suite is two floors of luxury living space connected by a delightful spiral staircase. Contemporary style furniture, handcrafted lamps and hardwood floors adorn the bedroom and living areas, accentuated by rich textiles and accessories. There is a separate spa bed/massage area and a private rooftop terrace with verdant garden and oversized plunge bath – an ideal spot to indulge yourself. Order an alfresco meal and enjoy a customised spa treatment or post-temple body massage for two within the privacy of your own rooftop hideaway.

Hotel Côté Cour SL

Beijing, China

An oasis of calm amid the commotion of Beijing

An exquisite synthesis of China's architectural heritage and the best in contemporary design, this 500-year-old *siheyuan* on Yanyue Hutong (Drama Music Lane) was where Ming dynasty actors rehearsed. In 2007, Shauna Liu an American citizen born in Bejing transformed it into the sleekest boutique hotel in the capital – the Côté Cour SL. For a *siheyuan*, it is in such glorious condition that it is a must see – sleeping here is a highly prized Beijing experience.

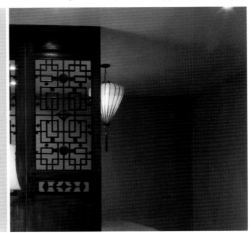

Traditional architectural features and interior details make this 500-year-old siheyaun *a oasis of peace in hectic Beijing.*

www.hotelcotecoursl.com

Our recommendation
Deluxe Room from $250 per night

Best time to visit	**May and June** **Early autumn is optimal**
Design style	**Traditional Chinese courtyard house experience with 21st century comforts**
Architects and designers	**Shauna Liu**

Antique black brick floors, black and white paintings on the walls and dark furniture contribute to the Ancient China atmosphere of the lounge.

Tones of red and black dominate both private and public spaces.

Once you have negotiated your way through the myriad of bicycles barrelling down the narrow hutong paths and solved the riddle of the confusingly numbered entrances, the suave embrace of the Orient welcomes you in the form of imposing double doors, painted red and complete with traditional lanterns and carved overhang.

Open the small door carved into one of the larger ones and experience the hospitality of an old Beijing home. The noise and confusion of the busy streets immediately vanish as you step into the intimate courtyard, so beautiful in its simplicity, centred round a rectangular decorative lily pond and a date tree and surrounded by the four buildings of the *siheyuan*, which seem to beckon you to a relaxing, almost spiritual encounter with the East.

Just to the left of the entrance, the front desk is located in a modern glass-enclosed room. Contemporary Chinese works of art adorn the walls of the only dining facility, the lounge, in careful contrast to the overall flavour of old China so masterfully recreated in 14 small yet magical rooms, all dressed in beautiful silks from southern China, with vibrant Tibetan carpets on antique black brick floors. Framed 'paper-cuts' and black-and-white photographs of hutongs line the soothing green walls, adding character to the cosy guest-rooms. Headboards engraved with Chinese poetry and sumptuous goose-down duvets and pillows welcome you to rest in the raised beds while rain showers seem to broaden the otherwise compact bathrooms. Should you wish to enjoy a slightly more generous living space and a plunge in a deep-soak bathtub, then opt for a Deluxe room, which still measures just 40 square metres.

Old Beijing is on your door step. Sit out on the roof-top deck to watch the goldfish sellers peddle their wares and glimpse the historic lane that was once home to artists of the imperial Ming court.

During the day the sights of The Forbidden City, Tiananmen Square and the Drum and Bell towers, all within walking distance, will tempt you, unless you prefer to take a stroll down Wangfujing, a renowned shopping street. In the evening, however, follow to the letter the suggestions of the hotel staff, who will guide you to the best dining and nightlife in the close-by hip Houhai Lake district.

A continental breakfast complete with Lavazza espresso is served in the lounge, where a lunch of traditional mouth-watering dim sum appears as if by magic at the appointed hour. And, as evening falls, cocktails are served in the subtle glow of dim floor lights while the country's customary red lanterns gently illuminate the courtyard.

Green Planet
Eco luxury resorts

Built in traditional Caribbean style from sustainable materials, each bungalow features a king-sized bed, a wrap around porch with lounge chairs and a personal beach-side hammock.

www.tiamoresorts.com

Our recommendation
Any of the 11 private beach-bungalows, from $630 per night

Best time to visit   **Mid October to end July**

Design style   **Traditional Caribbean style, rustic boutique**

Architects and   **Mike and Petagay Hartman**
designers

Tiamo

South Andros Island, Bahamas

Do everything, do nothing – welcome to the Bahamas

The brainchild of Mike and Petagay whose vision and passionate commitment made their dream a reality using only eco-friendly materials and equipment, Tiamo is a welcoming and laid back example of traditional Caribbean living. Arrive at the resort on South Andros Island, between the North and South Bights, and let the gentle pace help you unwind; let your worries fade away to the soothing sounds of the waves: there are no phones, TV or Internet here, only good company, good food and a host of close-to-nature activities.

Accessed by boat and with only 11 private beach-bungalow hideaways located on a wide stretch of 'slip through your toes' alabaster sand and warm, crystal-clear waters, this remote and romantic Caribbean eco-resort is an authentic and exclusive barefoot experience.

The experience

On the first morning, roll out of bed, saunter down to the water with a snorkel and swim out onto the Andros Barrier Reef to spy on hundreds of different types of marine life. Explore the tropical underwater landscape of the amazing off shore Blue Holes. Take a kayak to view the near shore marine life – starfish, conch, sea cucumber – then paddle on to explore the island's creeks, mangroves and natural habitats that teem with wildlife.

The pro-bono 'nature concierge team' will take you hiking into the 125 acres of protected wilderness to discover the many natural attractions; here you can spot wild orchid, giant cacti and glimpse the endangered Andros rock iguana.

Take in the beautiful and virtually untouched natural surroundings and would be eco-warriors can take pleasure in the knowledge that the entire resort uses less electricity in a month than the average UK or US household, helped in part by such energy efficient features as solar panels, elevated structures and white reflective roofs with wrap around porches that shield the interiors from the sun and enable cool breezes to blow through the buildings.

The main lodge is surrounded by sea grape trees and shady palms, dewy grass and flowers – it is here that you will eat, drink and socialise with the few other guests. Cocktails start at sundown followed by tantalising Caribbean cuisine. Local and highly sought after Bahamanian chefs have created a sophisticated dining experience based on classic Caribbean themes – savour the fresh rack of lamb with spicy, coconut infused rice or pineapple glazed Mahi with Caribbean couscous. All the dishes are prepared in a sustainable design state-of-the-art kitchen where spring-fresh reverse osmosis water cleans the greens while solar water heaters provide hot water for cooking and cleaning and power the refrigerators and freezers. Tiamo does not serve over-fished species in an effort to help preserve and build up remaining stocks.

For your eyes only

For complete indulgence treat yourself to a Swedish massage or detoxifying body scrub from the local masseuse to help you acclimatise to the island's gentle rhythms; then climb into a hammock and let the rest of the world drift away as you enjoy the serenity and breathe in the pure tropical air.

Each bungalow has a king-sized bed from which to enjoy the morning bird song and a wrap around terrace on which to sit and have your morning coffee served by the resort's highly attentive staff. To wash off the salt water, there's a spacious bathroom with beach rock shower floors and an open air vista.

Panoramic views of the Privassion Valley and waterfalls are just one of the dramatic experiences at this rustic-luxury eco property with organic gardens, waste water recycling and community involvement.

www.blancaneaux.com/

Our recommendation
The Enchanted Cottage from $1,200 per night

Best time to visit	**End November through to end of May**
Design style	**Luxury eco-lodge**
Architects and designers	**Eleanor Coppola and Francis Ford Coppola and Mexican architect Manolo Mestre**

Blancaneaux Lodge

Belize

A delicate balance of luxurious comfort and natural beauty – totally in harmony with its surroundings

With excellent access to some of Belize's most spectacular Mayan sites such as Caracol, Xunantunich, Pac Bitun and El Pilar, and an easily organised day trip across the border to Tikal and Yaxha in Guatemala, Blancaneaux Lodge is a luxurious and cultural jungle paradise.

Formerly his family's private retreat, Francis Ford Coppola opened his jungle Eden to the public as a fine example of a continually improving resort attentive to the conservation of the surrounding environment employing local resources, materials and personnel.

The experience
It doesn't market itself as a 'green resort', yet Blancaneaux Lodge has implemented many sustainable initiatives. For example, it supports Marcella Kelly of Virginia Tech's Department of Fisheries and Wildlife in her research on jaguars, puma and ocelot populations within the Chiquibul Forest Reserve, the 300 square miles of Mountain Pine Ridge Forest Reserve and the environs of Blancaneaux Lodge.

Blancaneaux Lodge grows over 80 per cent of its own organic vegetables and much of its fruit. It draws its energy from a self-sustaining, purpose built hydroelectric plant that harnesses the water power of Privassion Creek, which runs through the property.

The gardener and chef liaise daily to decide what produce is ready and what is needed for the freshly made dishes. There are two restaurants to choose from. The Montagna Restaurant offers an Italian-influenced menu while the Guatemaltecqua is for poolside eating. The Jungle Bar is adjacent to reception and open all day and evening. House wines served in the bar and restaurant are specially selected delicious organic vintages from the Coppola, Napa Rubicon Estate and from the new Francis Ford Coppola Presents, Rosso and Bianco winery in Sonoma.

For your eyes only
The Enchanted Cottage is the ultimate retreat. Situated on the edge of a steep forested bluff in a private and secluded part of the resort, it is the perfect hideaway and an ideal place to gather your thoughts, write that book, or paint a landscape inspired by the panoramic views of the tumbling waterfalls of Privassion Creek and the magnificent jungle-clad Maya Mountains in the distance. The screened porch, decking and infinity pool are surrounded by lush tropical gardens and native mixed forest of craboo, tropical oak and Caribbean pine.

Inside, items from Coppola's personal art and antiques collection are on display. The Bath House at the Enchanted Cottage has under floor heating, and an open fireplace and steam room. Luxuriate in the Japanese tub or rejuvenate aching limbs in the rainfall shower, before moving on to a great horse shoe shaped hot pool heated by excess energy from the hydroelectric plant and surrounded by heliconias and frangipani at the Waterfall Spa.

The Cottage enjoys the exclusive attention of an attendant, who will light the bathroom fire for you in the morning and cook you breakfast on the terrace. Let him organise private tours, horse riding and guided hikes around the property and out into the national park.

If, after the day's exertions, you don't feel like trying out the hot pool at of the Waterfall Spa and experimenting with the wide range of wraps and treatments available, your personal attendant can also arrange massages in the privacy of your Cottage – accommodation that truly lives up to its name!

Cusco's first entirely carbon-neutral hotel La Casona offers its guests an authentic eco-experience in the heart of a 16th-century colonial mansion, without compromises on comfort.

Inkaterra La Casona

Cusco, Peru

The perfect gateway to the Andes

Cusco's first entirely carbon-neutral hotel, with its mix of Old World history and New World comforts, Inkaterra La Casona is the perfect gateway to the Andes. A delightful re-imagining of an historic 16th-century colonial mansion in this ancient Pre-Colombian capital, it retains its original design and architecture around two open terraces on Plazoleta Las Nazarenas in the heart of the oldest quarter of Cusco.

Inkaterra as a group and La Casona in particular are committed to conservation and preservation and invest in renewable energy projects. They support local communities through responsible tourism initiatives including enabling guests to offset the greenhouse gas emissions caused by their air travel.

The experience
Tourists always receive a warm welcome in Cusco, where they can wander around the cobbled stone streets of the artists' district of San Blas, visit archaeological sites such as the Sacred Valley or simply spend time in the quaint local restaurants and craft shops.

At Inkaterra La Casona the carefully preserved patina of time and tradition provided by the colonial furnishings and original murals blends tastefully with modern comforts. In line with this, each of the 11 guestrooms has been given a contemporary twist, its technology sensitively concealed amid the historic frescos and fireplaces.

Plaza and Patio Suites overlook the city or internal terraces. They are furnished with beautiful antiques, have magnificent open fireplaces and king-sized beds dressed with down duvets and a cascade of pillows. Set around two inner private patios are separate living and dining rooms and large wide terraces equipped with comfortable day beds. The floors are heated throughout and the bathrooms are generously supplied with Inkaterra handmade toiletries to play with in your extra large bathtub and separate shower. There are in-room therapy tables for private massage and beauty treatments.

For your eyes only
For couples taking a romantic break let the concierge arrange for you to renew your vows with a regional shaman; or, for an out of the ordinary musical experience, surprise your partner with an Andean serenade by a colourful local group playing traditional instruments. The concierge can also organise any number of private tours of the area – and always accompanied by a gourmet picnic.

www.inkaterra.com/en/cusco

Our recommendation
The Plaza Suites from $940 per night

Best time to visit	**May to end September**
Design style	**Eco-chic, local and authentic**
Architects and designers	**Inkaterra**
Affiliation	**Inkaterra**

Posada de Mike Rapu

Easter Island, Chile

A dramatic and futuristic retreat

Wild plains, mysterious crater lakes, labyrinthine cave networks and giant stone statues all conspire to create an unforgettable environment for the traveller to explore from the comfort of Rapa Nui's first luxury lodge and South America's first green hotel.

The leading edge architecture of Posada de Mike Rapu relies entirely on indigenous materials to absorb the inspiration of the volcanic landscape into the design of the rounded central structure.

www.explora.com/rapa-nui_thehotel.php

Our recommendation
One of the four suites with stunning coastal views from $2,000 per night

Best time to visit	**December to February – a mild, sub-tropical climate all year**
Design style	**Futuristic, eco-friendly, local natural materials**
Architects and designers	**Jose Cruz Ovalle**
Affiliation	**Explora**

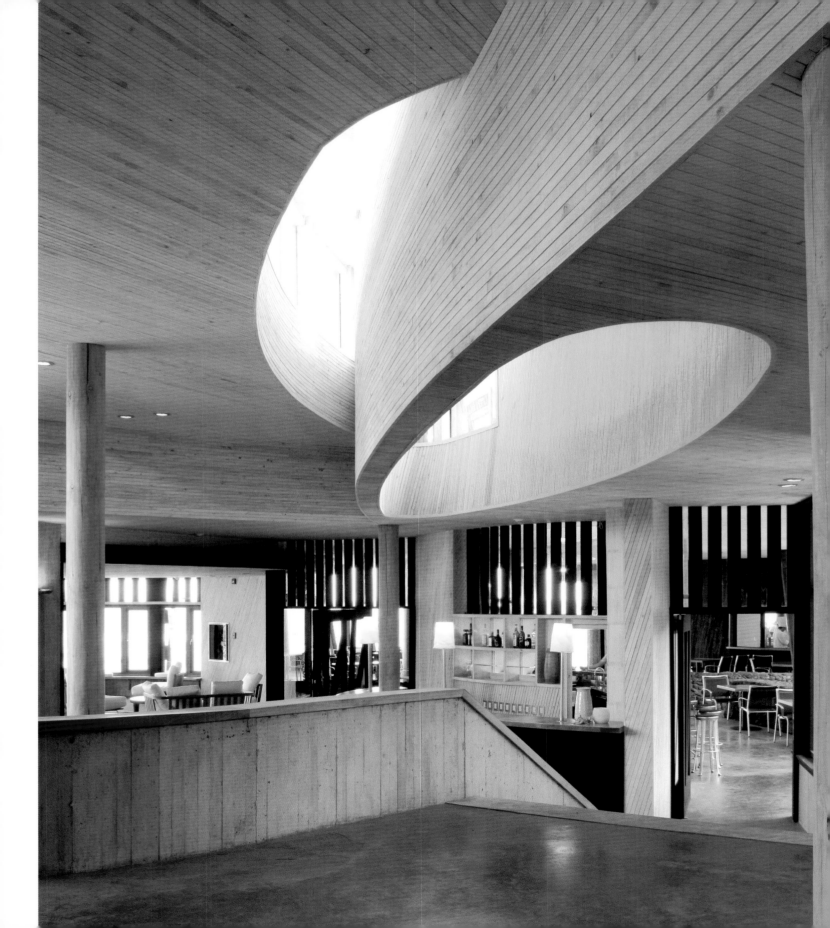

Opposite: The interior design of the lobby pays homage to the the volcanic origin of the island.
Above: Sustainably sourced pine and rauli wood feature extensively in the bedrooms and bathrooms.

Eco-conscious Explora group specialises in making accessible the fragility of the remote. At the same time Explora offers the means for sustaining local traditions and continually strives to preserve the quality of the environment it occupies.

On Easter Island particular attention should be devoted to the *ahus*, ceremonial burial platforms and vestiges of an ancient culture whose origins are shrouded in mystery. These are home to the famous sculptures that greet visitors upon arrival. Made of compressed volcanic ash, some up to 6 metres tall, with long faces, deep eye sockets and stoic expressions, they are the only survivors of an ancient civilisation.

Another guardian of the dramatic views over the Pacific and sitting low on the horizon is Posada de Mike Rapu. This spectacular retreat has been built as an eco-friendly initiative on the south shores and fashioned out of the ground using only local materials such as black lava, rauli wood and stone, rough-hewn pine and unpolished slate.

Inside, and the design round the central body of the property presents floors and ceilings of varying heights in homage to the surrounding volcanic landscape. Casa de Baños Hare Vai is situated to the side of the central body of general areas and has a pool, massage salon and open-air Jacuzzis.

All 30 guest rooms face the Pacific and are furnished in low-tech luxury using simple natural woods and materials, very soft and extremely comfortable. Bathroom interiors are of pine, the flooring and walls of local pizarra stone and the bespoke furniture is of rauli wood.

The restaurant has a glass-encased kitchen, which provides an excellent diversion from the spectacular landscape, allowing guests to watch as chefs prepare a delicious menu inspired by locally sourced healthy ingredients and served with excellent Chilean wines.

For a memorable experience have the bar tender make you a pisco sour, a Chilean cocktail blending brandy, lime and egg whites. Before you leave, don't forget to take a trip to the highest point on the island from where you can see the curvature of the earth before your very eyes.

Classic Africa where the experience is quintessentially beautiful and stunningly diverse.

The Fort

Onguma Game Reserve, Namibia

One of the most romantic settings in the world

Nature blew a kiss and planted it between the Kalahari and the South Atlantic calling it Namibia. Here in the dramatic Etosha Pans lies The Fort, set amid a romantic bush landscape of wild creatures and camel thorn trees and perhaps the most spectacular sunsets in Africa. Come and experience Africa from your personal castle.

Modern designer loungers and antique windows and doors go hand in hand at The Fort

www.onguma.com

Our recommendation
The Fort Suite from $430 per night

Best time to visit	**End April to end of November**
Design style	**Classic African with Moroccan and Indian accents**
Architects and designers	**Johan Slee, architect; Andre Louw, designer, Heidrun Diekmann, interior designer**
Affiliation	**Visions of Africa Safari Company**

From every area of the 12 suites, wooden decks lead towards the outside seating area and sun loungers for enjoying the spectacular views.

Northern Namibia is Africa's Next Great Safari Frontier in part owing to its incredible plethora of wildlife, but also because of its wealth of high-quality luxury lodges, like this camp on a private 50,000-acre game reserve, five minutes from Etosha National Park.

Unspoilt nature puts up a sensational show here and The Fort guests are invited to marvel at the 20,000 hectares of Onguma Game Reserve with two game drives a day. Watch over 30 different species of game including kudu, eland, Oryx, hartebeest and impala, their predators such as lion, leopard and cheetah, as well as the recently introduced family of black rhino and the multitude of bird species. Passionate bird watchers should not miss the summer months in Namibia when thousands of birds migrate to the wetlands after the seasonal rains.

The experience
With its antique windows and doors, billowy curtains and reflective pools,

The Fort features classical African design revisited with touches of Moroccan and Far Eastern influences. Through the dark cool rooms with artisan walls and high ceilings lie courtyards offering shade from the heat of the day and inviting you to sit and contemplate the calm to the gentle sound of the water feature.

A large and spacious communal guest lounge has a well stocked library and leads out to an open air dining room, which in turn extends through to a viewing deck and the outside. Here more romantic seating is available to sit with a cocktail in the raw beauty of the bush wilderness and watch the activity at the watering hole as giraffe, lion, zebra and hundreds of bird varieties come to drink and play in the cool of the evening and early in the morning as the sun rises.

There are 12 general suites adjacent to The Fort, each enjoying complete privacy with a master bedroom and dressing area and spacious ensuite bathrooms. All are open plan and have a private wooden deck for viewing across the Etosha Pan, but they all require you to lock yourself in at night, if you want to avoid the company of lions in the dark.

The Fort Suite is the only one locatd inside the main tower of the central Fort.

For your eyes only

The sunsets over Etosha Pan, the Jurassic Age lakebed between two and ten million years old, provide the memories of a lifetime. It bakes and shimmers in the height of the African sun and relies on annual rainfalls to keep the watering holes full. To see how nature supports this remarkable wildlife retreat is an extraordinary and life-changing experience.

There is no better spot to enjoy this than The Fort Suite, situated inside the main tower of the central Fort and featuring an enormous bathroom and bath to bathe in, long mirrors in distressed wooden frames and Middle Eastern lanterns. You can spy on your beautiful surroundings by gently lifting the canvas on the bedroom's walls to reveal mesh windows and, beyond those, safari paradise. Alternatively, move to the private viewing deck of your own open plan lounge or cool off in the lantern lit swimming pool. Wherever you chose to relax, the marvel of the protected wildlife and those sensational sunsets is never far away.

The Getty House rim-flow eternity pool.

Phinda
Private Game Reserve
KwaZulu-Natal, South Africa

Seven worlds of wonder

Meaning 'The Return' in Zulu, Phinda is an award-winning sustainable wilderness area spread over 23,000 hectares and covering the most diverse terrain, from rare dry sand forest to mountains, from marshes to savannah, where commitment to nature is matched by long-term investment in the local community.

Phinda means 'The Return' in Zulu and is an example of successful ecotourism, achieved by restoring misused farmland to a pristine state, restocking with the Big Five and other wildlife and developing it into an award winning, ecotourism destination.

www.phinda.com

Our recommendation
Phinda Mountain Lodge from $1,200 per night or Phinda Getty House from $5,800 per night. Combine some of the six lodges to truly experience Phinda

Best time to visit	**Subtropical climate – best game viewing from March to end September**
Design style	**Dramatic, Zulu Zen style**
Architects and designers	**Ridler Shepherd Louw; interiors: Chris Browne, CC Africa Creative Director**
Affiliation	**CC Africa**

Getty House is a gracious sole-use safari villa that overlooks an extinct volcano. Four spacious suites with sliding panel windows reveal sweeping views of the bushveld. Sandstone with timber, thatch and cement in construct provide airy free flowing spaces. Natural fibres and textures characterise the elegant interiors.

Travellers looking for a luxury safari enhanced by the feel good factor won't be disappointed. With its 23,000 hectares of conservation land in the lush Maputaland region of northern KwaZulu-Natal, South Africa, Phinda Private Game Reserve is a prime example of a remarkable initiative in environmental sustainability.

Here not only has misused farmland been restored to its pristine state, the Reserve restocked with the Big Five and key community projects funded, but a significant portion of the land itself has been returned to its ancestral owners so that they can now support the ongoing conservation and the biodiversity of the Reserve for generations to come.

The experience
Its impressive eco credentials aside, Phinda is an astonishing experience, offering seven distinct habitats in which to admire a wide variety of wildlife, from exotic birds, to rhinos, to the wild cats, as well as affording access by air to a spectacular marine ecosystem with unspoilt beaches at Sodwana and the stunning reefs of the Indian Ocean.

Choose to spend your stay at one of the six lodges, or simply travel between them under the knowledgeable direction of your own rangers and Zulu trackers to experience the rare dry sand forest at Vlei Lodge, with its glass encased suites on stilts, mountain views at Mountain Lodge and Rock Lodge, the lush valley at Zuka Lodge or the exclusive experience at Getty House.

Pan-African meals are prepared in a remarkable stone and reed *boma* (outdoor dining) and, in the evening, served romantically illuminated by dozens of candles and lanterns or moved to provide an open air banquet in a clearing in the bush – a spectacular setting under a sky of twinkling stars.

For your eyes only
At the new Mountain Lodge there are 25 split-level suites, each cresting the mountain's edge and offering breathtaking views of the Ubombo Mountains and the reserve below. A spacious private veranda, a plunge pool and romantic al fresco rain shower are complemented by the light chocolate and cream interiors and a collection of vintage Zulu beadwork.

Cosy guest sitting areas in shaded terraces, a three-tiered wraparound veranda and the observation deck simply deliver seductive comfort between each safari while offering spectacular views of the mountains and surrounding Zululand bushveld. Relaxation is further invited by the dramatic open-air *boma* and the cool, shaded swimming pool.

Overlooking an extinct volcano covered in lush vegetation and ringed by gentle hills, Phinda Getty House has been designed as a private residence for you to enjoy together with up to three other couples. Constructed of yellow sandstone, timber and thatch, the high ceilings and natural materials block the heat of the sun making the house airy, spacious and elegant. Interiors are simple but seriously stylish, incorporating natural fibres and materials such as grey slate and celadon. A private swimming pool and sun deck with wonderful views across the Reserve complete this superb property. The luxurious accommodation comes with a private ranger/host, tracker, butler and chef as well as exclusive use of an open 4x4 safari vehicle.

In this 1950s ambience, delicate Parsi tiles, woven hyacinth furniture and giant ebony chests provide the backdrop to an amazing experience in conservation on this legendary tiger circuit.

Baghvan
Luxury Wildlife Lodge
Pench National Park, India

Thrilling inspirations evocative of Kipling's *Jungle Book*

Baghvan is a mere five-minute drive from the wilderness of Pench National Park – part of the Bengal tiger circuit, which provided the inspiration for Rudyard Kipling's *Jungle Book*. Lodge guests can expect to be both enchanted and enthralled by their surroundings. The forested areas teem with birds – over 300 species have been recorded here – while wildlife include the illusive tiger, leopard, wolf, chital, sambar, muntjac, langur and rhesus macaque, all of which can be spotted roaming the jungle. Guests enjoy twice-daily safaris in the reserve in a specially designed Tata 4x4.

Baghvan comprises 12 individual suites, each with two inter-linked buildings accessed via a courtyard. Decorated in shades of copper with hues of pale turquoise and cream, the bedrooms are beautiful (and air conditioned). The bathrooms feature distinctive indoor and outdoor shower areas and every suite has a private roof top terrace for game watching, stargazing and, if guests so desire, a romantic night under the heavens.

www.tajsafaris.com

Our recommendation
All 12 individual suites $820 per night

Best time to visit	**Optimal, October through to June** **low season, mid-April to end June** **Closed July to end September**
Design style	**Retro 50s safari style ambiance**
Architects and designers	**Taj Hotels in collaboration with CC Africa**
Affiliation	**Taj Hotels Resorts and Palaces, CC Africa, Chris Browne**

Set 200 metres out over the Indian Ocean, the two Ocean Pavilions are the ultimate luxury on the island.
The private fibre-optic lit infinity pool flows from the indoors out and merges seamlessly with the horizon.

Huvafen Fushi

Maldives

A waking dream

If your idea of paradise is a pristine and tranquil tropical island with swaying palms, pure white sands and a brilliant azure lagoon combined with luxurious and contemporary accommodation, then Huvafen Fushi, at the end of its 650 foot jetty, is your perfect destination.

www.huvafenfushi.com

Our recommendation
The Beach Pavilion with private pool from $5,000 for seven nights or an Ocean Pavilion with private pool from $4,700 for seven nights

Best time to visit	**December to end April**
Design style	**Contemporary**
Architects and designers	**Carl Ettensperger, C&C Studio; underwater treatment rooms at LIME spa: Richard Hywel Evans Architecture and Design**
Affiliation	**Per Aquum Resorts Spas Residences**

Restaurant Celsius, the main infinity pool and the salt water floatation pool Lonu Veyo are all within easy reach.

Huvafen Fushi strives hard to deserve its green credentials, actively supporting carbon offset programmes, using fair trade products and participating in community education programmes. The resort cooperates with VSO Maldives and the Educational Development Centre so that an overseas teacher can assist local school staff on a remote atoll.

A coral Reef Rehabilitation Project is working on Huvafen Fushi's own reef overseeing the successful restoration of ecosystems and starting a coral nursery, monitored by a resident marine biologist and her own 'Green Team'. To make their own contribution, guests are invited to adopt selected baby coral and transplant it on to the reef.

The experience
Sample the island's many activities from wine tastings to dancing to the music of visiting DJs or playing football on the beach with staff. Charter the 70ft luxury yacht *Sensuelle*, complete with its own private spa, and take her out to explore the 1,190 coral islands that make up the Maldives. Sail to any

number of world-class scuba dives and investigate the reefs and marine life. Lazy days are easily filled with a myriad activities on land and sea . . .

And when it comes to wining and dining, guests are really spoilt for choice: try Celsius, an easy going luxe-but-laid-back dining experience situated over the lagoon and offering a range of sensational dishes; vegetarians will love Raw, the healthy stop for enjoying 'Spa and Raw' with a juice bar for exquisite mixes; and then there's UMbar, a well stocked venue on the water's edge where you can sink into a beanbag and watch the sunset over designer cocktails. As its name suggests, Vinum holds regular wine tastings and has a subterranean wine cellar with over 800 vintages. And after all that indulgence, there's an air-conditioned gym to keep up your fitness regime; or, for those after something a little more downbeat, a yoga pavilion with daily classes to rebalance and energise the soul.

For your eyes only
The all white underwater treatment rooms at the Lime Spa offer an exclusive experience and the perfect environment to indulge in a massage. Specialising in water therapies (of course) and delicious Li' Tya facials, your gaze will be transfixed by the brightly coloured parrotfish, the ribbon-like fins of lionfish and the tentacles of octopus as they glide gently past your nose. Choose from

The Beach Pavilion is blessed with an infinity pool that flows from inside out towards the ocean, overlooked from the master bedroom above through a glass floor.

six Energy Rituals specifically designed for Lime. From holistic to sublime these treatments are tailored to you alone and incorporate local virgin coconut oil – hypnotic seduction at its finest.

The Ocean Pavilions with private pool have sunset views and are the ultimate in pampered luxury above the water. Secluded and only accessed by you, there is a fibre-optic lit infinity pool which merges with the horizon. An open plan master bedroom has an infinity edge Kohler bath that is filled from the ceiling and forms the centrepiece. A dedicated *thakuru* (butler) ensures your every need is met, filling your bathtub, organising deep sea diving expeditions or simply opening the bottle of Veuve Clicquot stashed in your fridge.

On land and the ultimate experience is the Beach Pavilion with its private pool and beach. Organised on two levels, this is a gem of avant-garde design with signature furniture pieces by Frank Gehry. The master bedroom has an oversized king bed and offers views through the glass floor down into the infinity pool and out onto the lagoon. Your private outdoor oasis has an open-air shower and the gardens encase your outsized bath. A dining room overlooks the entry ponds and an expansive fibre-optic pool flows from inside the pavilion to the outside.

The interiors of the world's first underwater spa have been influenced by the colours and textures of the sea to create a relaxing, dreamlike environment.

Red Capital Ranch

Beijing, China

A former Manchurian hunting estate from the Qing Dynasty

Beijing's most extraordinary eco-tourism resort is a former Manchurian hunting lodge set in a private valley estate of 50 acres. Painstakingly restored by the same master craftsmen who were entrusted with the repair of the fabled Forbidden City, The Ranch's architecture is inspired by Manchu, Mongolian and Tibetan Buddhist cultures. A highly privileged setting, it acts as 'guardian' with exclusive access to a protected gate opening onto one of the few remaining wonders of the world – the Great Wall of China.

Sparse, colourful furniture embellish the rustic interiors of the villas, priviledged guardians of the Great Wall.

www.redcapitalclub.com.cn/ranch.html

Our recommendation
One of two extra large suites with roof top from $250 per night

Best time to visit   **March to November (closed from December to mid March)**

Design style   **Authentic Chinese, Tibetan and Manchurian elements**

Architects and designers   **Red Capital and a team of specialist artisans**

The 10 individual residences are laid out in historical military manner and furnished in a colourful traditional Manchurian style.

Opened in 2004 as the perfect 'eco-tourism escape', the Ranch is the brainchild of Laurence Brahm, the well-connected American entrepreneur, lawyer and writer who had previously created restaurant Red Capital Club and boutique hotel Red Capital Residence in Beijing.

Reverence for nature, a cornerstone of both Buddhism and Taoism, is everywhere evident. From each one of the ten highly individual residences inspired by the hunting lodges of the Qing emperors Kangxi and Qianlong, guests are treated to views of the Great Wall, of the surrounding mountains and of the picturesque rivers that meander through this unique estate. The original hunting lodge, animal sighting pavilion and stables date back to the first emperor Qin Shi Huangdi. Today, these ancient structures have been sympathetically 'refashioned' by the same artisans responsible for repairs to the Forbidden City. The hunting lodge is now a fine dining restaurant that offers gourmet cuisine

taking influences from sophisticated Manchu, Mongolian and Tibetan specialities including Oriental delicacies to tempt even the most world weary traveller. On balmy summer and autumn evenings the open air animal sighting pavilion enables diners to savour those highly seductive views over a glass of wine.

Across the courtyard lies the Warlord's Lounge, decorated in a nostalgic 1950s' style. A tribute to Wu Peifu, one of China's most notorious warlords, his violent career is captured in the calligraphy of the time, which recounts his rampages across the country during the Republican period (1911-49).

Next door is the Tibetan Tiger Lounge housing the bar, dominated by the glorious wooden door with a tiger motif, from a 19th-century Tibetan temple, and the enormous open stone fireplace. Here logs burn and golden tigers leap as sparks crackle and fly on chilly nights and winter days – ideal for sitting over a drink and contemplating the magnificent views of The Great Wall.

Each room is protected by an animal spirit carved in antique stone, dating back to the early Qing Dynasty.

For your eyes only

The newly built Tibetan Secret Spa is a quiet haven and serves only one or two people at a time. After a hard day's Wall climbing, drift off with a soothing and recuperative Five Elements massage based on ages' old Chinese philosophy and incorporating the five elements: earth, wood, fire, water and gold. Complementing your massage, the therapist starts with Earth – two warm stones, black and white representing yin and yang – which you hold in your hands as aids to meditation while she works on those aching joints. Wood follows (as Earth nourishes Wood), and incense from Tibetan medicinal herbs is burned, enhancing the relaxing atmosphere and balancing your yin and yang. Then comes Fire – a single candle is lit in your honour; finally, when the main treatment is complete, Water – and a Ginseng tea to nourish your vital qi energies. As a coda, gold or metal is reflected in an ancient sensory massage that focuses on key acupuncture points to release vital energy, reduce stress and rejuvenate, restoring internal balance.

Each of the 10 distinctive villas is designed, positioned and protected by name to evoke an ancient eight-trigram battle array (when soldiers drew their power and style of fighting from nature's inspiration). Water, Thunder, Wind, Mountain, Heaven, Lade, Yin and Yang, Fire and Earth. Built in a combination of stone, wood and brick, the villas house unique artefacts, bridgehead stones and carvings, wood sculptures from the Ming Dynasty and stone animals from the Quin Dynasty. While structure and decor are beautifully preserved in a classical style, bathrooms and technology are state of the art and, for your added pleasure, are plentifully supplied with a range of choice teas, handmade Chinese cassia soaps and natural ginseng shampoos.

Let the restaurant arrange a picnic for you on your Great Wall and other excursions – there are so many sights worth taking in from your Ranch location. Visit the Hidden Lake and the garden house of Madame Song, wife of Sun Yatsen and mother of the last emperor Pu Yi. Take a guided tour to the Secret Temples and see the largest Confucian temple, hidden away in an ancient hutong by the famous Hanlin Academy where once Qing scholars sat their imperial examinations.

Stellar Resorts
Sea, sports, spas and safaris

Sanctuary
on Camelback Mountain
Arizona, USA

Physical and spiritual rejuvenation in a paradise valley

Its clean modern design complementing the tones and textures of the rugged Arizona surroundings, the award winning Sanctuary at Camelback Mountain offers guests the opportunity to enjoy a myriad of outdoor pursuits and state of the art spa treatments, and for some provides the answer to their search for physical and spiritual nourishment.

The soothing colours of the Sanctuary Spa promise relaxation and wellbeing.

www.sanctuaryoncamelback.com

Our recommendation
Spa Casita Suite from $650 per night in 2008

Best time to visit	**September to June**
Design style	**Contemporary boutique resort that draws design influences from the natural rugged mountainous landscapes and sunny desert environs**
Architects and designers	**Allen + Philp Architects**

Opposite: The spacious living room with panoramic views of CasaTen.

Above: A glimpse of life in Casa Montana, with its private outdoor pool, master bedroom and lounge with snooker table.

In the middle of the Arizona desert these 53 acres of Sanctuary boutique hideaway shimmer like an elusive oasis set on the northern slope of Camelback Mountain's distinctive red rockface.

A former tennis clubhouse come casitas designed by Frank Lloyd Wright protégé Hiram Hudson Benedict in 1950, the resort has since reinvented itself a number of times, changing names and ultimate goals.

The experience
Sport, wellbeing and relaxation are at the heart of the philosophy of the Sanctuary that now features the largest infinity pool in Arizona, a state of the art indoor/outdoor Asian-inspired spa and a meditation garden.

An endless choice of recreational activities is provided, from horseback riding, hiking and biking in the desert to tennis on one of the five championship courts and golf at Paradise Valley's renowned courses. World-class shopping and museums are a mere 20 minutes away.

The 7 mountainside estates @ Sanctuary and 98 mountain and spa casitas offer spacious rooms or suites with contemporary furnishing, wood block flooring and original works of art to complement the overall mood and landscape. Some feature wood burning fireplaces and outdoor viewing terraces and all contain canopied bedrooms and large travertine marble bathrooms, equipped with oversized tubs and separate showers.

Executive chef Beau MacMillan oversees an American cuisine with Asian accents to provide a sophisticated menu at signature restaurant elements. Adjacent is jade bar, an indoor/outdoor gathering place with an extensive wine cellar. Try the Cantaloupe Martini, a Sanctuary signature cocktail.

With its Watsu immersion pool for hydro-treatments alongside 12 general treatment rooms and a Zen Meditation Garden, the Sanctuary Spa has created a haven of peace and relaxation in a sleek contemporary setting.

For your eyes only
Book the Spiral 'yin' and 'yang' Sanctum outdoor treatment room for two for instant access to vitality pools, fire pits, deluge showers and spa therapies, all in total privacy. Or try the Satori programme specially designed to promote tranquillity and rejuvenation.

For a true ultraluxe experience, out of the seven mountainside estates @ Sanctuary, book Casa 9. Here a serene courtyard welcomes guests into the main house, its décor in soft earth tones set off by a stunning flagstone fireplace. The grandmaster suite is huge with a big bed and ensuite bathroom. Outside there are two private pools, one with a swim-up bar and a Jacuzzi. Original sculptures in the gardens add the finishing touch.

At Capella Castlemartyr guests can discuss the myths of the Knights Templar in the ruins of their castle, indulge in the state-of-the-art
Auriga spa with ozone-pool and let the Irish setters Earl and Countess take them for walks around the estate.

Capella Castlemartyr

County Cork, Ireland

Return to an era of castles and knights on a romantic estate

Irish charm and culture epitomised, this 220-acre estate encompasses the vast greenery of Mitchell's Woods and the dramatic ruins of an ancient castle built in 1210, enjoyed a few hundred years later by Elizabeth I's favourite Sir Walter Raleigh, until the fourth Earl of Shannon took possession of the estate.

The decor of this 17th-century manor is understated opulence – this is timeless elegance Irish-style that flows seamlessly from the main house and into the new wing. Lavish and gracious interiors have original oak floors strewn with Persian rugs, double layered damask silk curtains at the windows and antiques in every room.

Chef Roger Ohlsson was coaxed from London's prestigious Michelin starred Pied à Terre to the Bell Tower, the hotel's fine dining room, its three rooms overlooking the delights of the formal gardens. Here, Ohlsson serves cuisine prepared with the best local farm fresh ingredients and herbs from the castle's own herb garden.

Beautiful scenery, unrivalled comfort and gourmet dining are complemented by Auriga, Capella's signature spa, located in an eye-catching modern structure adjacent to the manor house, and in perfect keeping with the estates, architectural heritage. Experience one of the three 'vanishing edge' vitality pools or the magnificent ozone-treated pool with its extraordinary sparkling water for a most unusual swim. Alternatively, treat yourself and your partner to a bit of Irish magic in a private VIP suite with the signature Auriga treatment based on the phases of the moon, an approach credited with bringing enhanced awareness of the rhythms of nature and increased wellbeing.

The estate offers plenty of opportunities for recreation. Created by renowned golf course designer Ron Kirby, an 18-hole inland links-style course promises to be the perfect challenge for golfers, while wellingtons have been thoughtfully provided for guests who enjoy long walks, setting out over the trimmed lawns to wade through the streams that crisscross the property. Take a picnic lunch out in a horse-drawn carriage and go for a leisurely ride around the grounds or simply wrap yourself in the cashmere blankets, grab a mug of mulled wine and relax in the outdoor loungers besides log fire pits.

www.capellacastlemartyr.com/

Our recommendation
Book a Grand Suite, located in the 17th-century manor house from $1,560 per night

Best time to visit	**All year – optimum June to September and October for the jazz and film festivals**
Design style	**Classic Irish-style country manor house – gracious and comfortable**
Architects and designers	**MDM, International, San Diego and Jack Coughlans Associates, Cork – architects. Peter Silling, Hotel Interior Design (HID)**
Affiliation	**Capella Hotels and Resorts**

Terme Manzi has an Epicurean wellness centre with a dramatic indoor thermal pool and treatment rooms on the island of Ischia.

Terme Manzi Hotel & Spa
Ischia, Italy

The heart of Ischia

Said to have cured the legendary Ulysses and Italian patriot Garibaldi and to have fortified such notable devotees as Lamartine and Ibsen, the mineral rich volcanic waters of the Gurgitiello springs have long been famous for their health giving properties. The modern day hotel's spa is situated directly above these waters and guests can enjoy customised treatments.

Manzi Terme, the premiere '*terme*' on Ischia is blessed with warm sunny summers and balmy winters. The island has some of the Mediterranean's most golden beaches and is surrounded by a piercing aquamarine sea.

The experience
From the entrance on Piazza Bagni di Gurgitiello, walk past the 18th-century mosaics, crystals and sculptures into the grand hall whose ceiling retains its original architectural details. Wander out into the courtyards and gardens with their marble fountains – a haven of olive trees, vines and orange trees. Sip a drink on the panoramic terrace and gaze down onto the thermal pool's mosaic walls that reflect the colours of sun and sea. Rooms too have a Mediterranean charm, with carefully matching furnishing and fabrics, marine stencils on the walls and tiled floors in the bathrooms. And from the windows in this sea front location, guests enjoy panoramic views.

There are several dining options; for gourmets there is Il Mosaico where young local chef Nino di Constanzo takes traditional Italian recipes and translates them into exquisitely presented modern classics – the seafood is unsurpassed.

For your eyes only
The Spa is designed in Pompeian style with columns and vaulted ceilings, mosaics and waterfalls. Every guest is given a full assessment so a customised treatment programme can be devised combining '*terme*' experiences with therapeutic or aesthetic treatments and an appropriate diet and exercise regime. All treatments use natural ingredients and have been scientifically conceived. Manzi Terme adheres to the classical philosophy of Epicureanism – in life derive the greatest amount of pleasure, yet do so with moderation in order to avoid the suffering incurred by overindulgence. Unnecessary and, especially, artificially produced desires are to be suppressed. The Spa approaches body and spirit in this way too.

www.termemanzihotel.com

Our recommendation
Take a suite from $1,165 per night

Best time to visit	**April to October**
Design style	**Luxury Pompeian**
Architects and designers	**Cesare Luongo** **lighting system in the indoor pool and in the courtyard: Nord Light**

Kasbah Tamadot

Atlas Mountains, Morocco

A warm Berber welcome

A truly exotic location, Kasbah Tamadot has been sensitively transformed from its feudal roots into a delightful partnership of Berber and European design. Traditional methods have been used to create a building that honours the Toubkal National Park environment in which it sits to provide the perfect setting from which to explore the entire country.

Kasbah Tamadot is a magical walled citadel where authentic Moroccan charm is infused with contemporary chic.

www.kasbahtamadot.virgin.com

Our recommendation
Deluxe suite with pool from $1,042

Best time to visit	**April to early January**
Design style	**Traditional Moroccan infused with contemporary elements**
Architects and designers	**Virgin Limited Edition**
Affiliation	**Virgin Limited Edition**

The Master Suite is set apart from the other accommodations, across the gardens. It has three bedrooms and a private pool and enjoys full views of the nearby mountains.

Kasbah Tamadot – 'soft breeze' in Berber – is a former feudal Caïd in the foothills of Jbel Toubkal, in the North African Atlas Mountains. In 1998 Richard Branson's mother fell in love with it during one of his round the world balloon attempts and convinced him to purchase it from owner Luciano Stanco, as a fitting addition to its luxury retreat collection.

The experience

Leaving the sounds and smells of a hectic Marrakech, guests are collected by luxury limousine and transferred in some 45 minutes to their romantic destination. Here they can simply slip on their *babouches* and, after a traditional and very refreshing mint tea, take a walk to explore the hotel interiors, blissfully encased within Kasbah Tamadot's protective walls. A leisurely wander around is rewarded by the sight of an intriguing maze of courtyards, rooms and staircases, set in extensive grounds and exquisitely landscaped gardens with rose, fruit and cactus plants.

Pre-dinner cocktails at the intimate fire-side bar are the perfect entrée to Kanoun restaurant, a real treat for the taste buds serving delicious local produce and flavours combined with continental ideas. The team of chefs prepare fresh baked ksra bread and tagines cooking on free-standing clay charcoal braziers – the *kanouns* from which the restaurant takes its name – are an absolute must. Spices and dried fruits from Marrakech, fish fresh from the Atlantic, vegetables from the local fields and out of this world 'free-range' meats are accompanied by a superlative wine and champagne list. In the summer, dine in a private courtyard under the stars or on the spectacular roof terrace.

Each of the 18 rooms is individually decorated, spacious, warm in winter and cool in summer and each features a king-size bed and either a Moroccan-style bathroom with the traditional arched entrance and sunken bathing area or a contemporary bathroom with a free-standing bathtub and overhead rain shower.

For your eyes only

Wash off your traveller's dust with a traditional Moroccan hammam in the Asoufou spa. A heated outdoor infinity pool shares its space and affords panoramic views of the mountains; on chillier autumn evenings a dip in the heated indoor pool is a perfect retreat.

Beduin-style tents and genuine Berber staff from local villages add some authenticity to the whole experience.

If you wish, you can gaze at the Atlas Mountains from a hot air balloon – leaving at sunrise and chasing the sun to view the spectacular and mesmerising landscape below as you soar as high as an eagle. Down to earth and mule riding can be organised: a professional guide will escort you and your steeds into the mountains for an unforgettable trek.

Book a Deluxe Suite with a separate sitting room and a private terrace or mini-courtyard – if you can compromise on space, ask for one of the higher suites with stunning panoramic views; alternatively, opt for a larger space and a suite tucked away on the ground floor.

Salam alikoum – peace be with you.

Despite temperatures here are at least 10 degrees cooler than in Marrakesh in the summer, the warm waters of the outdoor infinity pool are inviting and rinvigorating.

Desert Palm is the ultimate luxury polo retreat where guests can enjoy watching the game while eating al fresco or taking tea.

Desert Palm

Dubai, United Arab Emirates

Chic luxury rising from a dramatic desert landscape

Arabian horses gallop across the lush green polo field, as players compete for points in the chukka – Desert Palm is the ultimate ultraluxe polo retreat and a chic oasis for visitors.

Situated just outside Dubai and away from the frenetic bustle of the city centre, Desert Palm is suffused with both the natural energy of these elegant beasts and the essence of the mystical desert in which it lies.

Polo is obviously the main attraction at Desert Palm: there are four championship polo fields, stabling for over 300 horses and a riding school which allows riders access over the 150 verdant acres of the estate. The resort, however, is set apart from the equestrian areas and is an exclusive enclave with the ambience of a private home comprised of 24 'naturally modern' chic suites and pool villas offering total privacy and set in this glorious and peaceful sanctuary. Each home showcases individual elegance realised in neutral colours and embodies the simplicity and timelessness of the estate's graceful palm trees and green fields.

The experience
If you can tear yourself away from your favourite sport, dine at Rare, a restaurant in an elevated position that affords views on the surrounding fields from both inside and on the terrace. Delicately prepared wood-fired steaks are a speciality and whether your preference from the beech oven and grill is Kobe, Black Angus, Wagyu or Argentinean Chimichurri, all are on offer in succulent form. Game and line-caught seafood also feature on this selectively cosmopolitan menu, accompanied by premium vintages from both the Old and the New Worlds.

Alternatively, sample the excellent range of connoisseur coffees and teas as well as various gastronomic temptations at Epicure, the gourmet deli café next to the infinity pool. Its air-conditioned seating overlooking the pool, palms and vibrant green fields, makes this an ideal venue from which to enjoy the horsemanship and the antics in the pool.

Lime spa and wellness boutique, a spiritual space that echoes the colours, textures and aromas of the Arabian landscape, completes the Desert Palm experience. Design your exclusive journey of discovery, fusing Asian and European therapies and massages as well as Lime's own signature treatments customised for each client with a range of energising rituals that introduce crystals, mineral healing and aromatic essences. A source of relaxation, fitness and healthy organic cuisine.

For your eyes only
Book one of the Pool Residences, and revel in your very own secluded Arabian oasis, complete with private garden large swimming pool, outdoor dining area and sunbathing deck. The ultimate 'home away from home'.

www.desertpalm.ae

Our recommendation
Pool Residence from $1,540 per night

Best time to visit	**November to April**
Design style	**Arabia with touches of the avant-garde**
Architects and designers	**AR+D Singapore architects, IMA interiors Singapore**
Affiliation	**Small Luxury Hotels of the World**

The outdoor deck is the perfect place to admire the striking views of the mountain that rise above the Thimphu Valley.

Taj Tashi
Thimphu, Bhutan

Revel in National Happiness

The land of the thunder dragon, mystical Bhutan is one of the most unspoilt cultures of the modern world. Steeped in the ancient ways of Mahayana Buddhism, its practices permeate every aspect of Bhutanese life and art. For the visitor this tiny kingdom offers spectacular monasteries, centuries-old street festivals and miles of wilderness and mountain scenery to marvel at and explore. Thimphu is the capital of this serene, almost secret Himalayan country and the ideal base for exploring it.

www.tajhotels.com

Our recommendation
One of the corner suites on the fourth floor, which are both spacious and have the best views. From $600 per night

Best time to visit	**March to May and September to early December**
Design style	**Inspired by Bhutan's dzong architecture with contemporary touches**
Architects and designers	**Carl Almeida, P49 deesign, Bangkok**
Affiliation	**Taj Hotels Resorts and Palaces**

Magnificent, sculptural interiors reflect the origins of this former fortress-monastery.

Taj Tashi is the first luxury hotel permitted to open its doors in the heart of the capital of this fledgling democracy. Reflecting the *dzong* style architecture, thanks to its position the hotel dominates the skyline in what is a low-rise city.

A truly dramatic boutique hotel, as you enter you will be struck by the beautifully intricate murals depicting traditional emblems of clouds, double *dorjes* (symbolic thunderbolts) and *dhungs* (horn-like musical instruments).

The experience
There are 66 guest rooms, each elegantly appointed to reflect the region's art and colour in a happy mix of traditional and contemporary styles: hand-painted walls with ceiling motifs, lattice panelling of blue pine and beautiful rugs on the floors.

Chig-ja-gye is the restaurant that serves excellent Bhutanese cuisine: sit and enjoy steamed dumplings, or *ema datshi*, Bhutan's national dish of firey green chillies in cheese sauce accompanied by red rice and served with a touch of 'Taj finesse'. After a hard day exploring, take tea at Rimps and choose from a soothing selection of teas including butter tea, a first for Western palates and a local favourite. Before dinner the Ara Lounge Bar provides the perfect setting to enjoy a pre-dinner drink.

The Taj Spa entices guests into a serene environment where ancient and mystic healing arts come together to create unique indulgence. The spa-sanctuary overlooks a swimming pool, sun deck and landscaped surroundings. Timeless Bhutanese architecture and hand-painted art blend with nature to impart a sense of harmony, balance and wellbeing. The wet area encompasses a steamroom, sauna, heated swimming pool and a Jacuzzi. And for those in search of exercise there is a good-sized gym for early morning sessions.

For your eyes only
At the Taj Spa, there are a myriad of Bhutanese and Indian treatments to choose from that heal, detoxify and revitalise body and mind. Book a spa suite and try one of the signature treatments such as Manda Snānā, a special 'Bhutanese Hot Stone Bath', which will relieve aching muscles and stiffness, and revive and re-hydrate the body.

If you feel fit and able, you can't miss the hike to Tiger's Nest, Bhutan's most sacred monasteriy, reputedly first set up by Guru Rinpoche who flew here on a tigress in the 8th century. Its striking white building with red adornments and gold cupola roof is perched on the far side of a deep canyon, precariously nestled into a steep cliff face nearly 600 metres above the forest floor.

The famous Tiger Nest monastery is within reach of Taj Tashi's guests.

Traditional Vietnamese architecture merges with sleek contemporary design.

The Nam Hai

Hoi An, Vietnam

Where heaven and earth changed places

Vietnam is a country staggering in its beauty. Here soaring peaks cloaked in mysterious mists clear to reveal dense forests concealing ancient temples and a rich variety of wildlife. Lush green paddi fields are laid out like the squares on a chessboard, its pieces are women tending the fields in their conical hats. Bright, vibrant colours in nature are reflected in the people whose country – contrary to misguided notions – is now one of the safest, most hospitable places on the planet.

www.ghmluxuryhotels.com/NamHai.htm

Our recommendation
A Beachfront Pool Villa from $850 per night

Best time to visit	**May to October – optimum late March to July**
Design style	**Traditional Vietnamese with Chinese and Japanese influences**
Architects and designers	**Architecture: AW2** **interiors and furnishing: Jaya Ibrahim and Jaya & Associates** **landscaping: KPD**
Affiliation	**GHM Luxury Hotels**

The spa stretches over two buildings connected by a bridge.

Home to the biggest US airforce base in Vietnam at the time of the infamous conflict over 30 years ago, Danang has successfully reinvented itself in recent years and its airport now serves some of the most luxurious holiday resorts in the area. With its 100 designer villas, the Nam Hai is one of the newest and most elegant additions on this horseshoe-shaped spit of sand.

Here the understated charm of Vietnamese architecture – split level accommodation, slanted roofs and wooden platforms – subtly blends with elements of contemporary designer chic – dark woods against white walls, symmetrical architecture, infinity pools and faultless lawns. And to frame it all, the calm waters of three pools, sandy beaches and the stunning seafront.

Behind the success of such a venture is the collaboration of the biggest names in hotel design of recent years: founder Adrian Zecha, French architect Reda Amalou and Indonesian interior designer Jaya Ibrahim.

The experience
The Spa is an enticing sanctuary set away from the villas, around the lagoon just off the beach. Eight treatment pavilions are located in two separate buildings, linked by a delicate bridge spanning a lotus flower pond.

At the restaurant, Australian head chef Kath Townsend is already winning accolades for her talent in cooking a variety of cuisines from all regions of the world and keeping flavours true to their origin. She focuses on fresh local seasonal produce to ensure the dishes are of the finest of quality.

Definitely worth a visit is Hoi An, a 16th-century commercial port just seven miles away from Nam Hai. A World Heritage site, the town has preserved much of its orginal architecture, especially in the French quarter. With 400 tailors to chose from, it is also the tailoring capital of Vietnam. If you have time, take a trip to Hue, the ancient Nguyen Dynasty capital.

Decadent Pool Villa and heavenly pool.

Asian-fusion cuisine in sublime surroundings has won many awards.

For your eyes only

If the one-bedroomed villas are far too small for your needs, opt for one of the 40 delightfully decadent Pool Villas, which come equipped with traditional sloping roof, up to five bedrooms and a dedicated butler or maid. Utmost care has been taken to harmonise with nature so each villa is designed and laid out along traditional Vietnamese lines. On the ground floor, there are open spaces and access to the garden and pool. Two steps up, on the next level, are the sleeping quarters, with massive king-sized beds dressed in sumptuous Irish linens. In the evening, as soon as your butler draws the delicate silk curtains, your room acquires an aetherial quality. Lights are dimmed, candles lit and romantic music is carried on the breeze as the ocean waves break gently on the shore.

Bathing here is a divine experience as bathrooms are furnished with an extra large, exquisite, handmade eggshell-lacquer bathtub for two. Sink into its scented waters with a glass of champagne and enjoy privacy Vietnamese style, protected from view by intricately carved Oriental screens and the finest silks.

The view across the infinity pool towards the ocean is calm and serene.

The Fortress

Galle, Sri Lanka

The ultimate relaxation

Built in the style of a powerful fortress blending historic Dutch and Portuguese influences with original Sri Lankan motifs, The Fortress rises imposingly at the water's edge, its walls enclosing exquisitely appointed rooms, lofts and residences where guests are cocooned in a dreamy water world.

www.thefortress.lk

Our recommendation
**The Loft Rooms from $800 per night and
The Fortress Residence from $1,700 per night**

Best time to visit	**Optimum from December to end April**
Design style	**Historic Ceylon meets modern Asia**
Architects and designers	**C&C, Singapore**
Affiliation	**Per Aquum Resorts Spas Residences Small Luxury Hotels of the World**

Contemporary design and technology are integral to this colonially inspired fortress. Guests can take tea on the terrace; drink in the view from the sunken lounge; play in their personal den or sip cocktails in the bar area.

Fashioned in the style of a powerful fortress and rising next to the sea, The Fortress walls enclose exquisitely appointed rooms, lofts and residences.

The design of the six Ocean Lofts is in the guise of a split-level space creating unique experiences on each floor. Guests enter an oversized living room with indoor plunge pool and inviting day bed. The upstairs level houses the bedroom, with a luxury bed made up with soft Egyptian cotton Frette linen. The stunning upstairs bathroom features both rainfall and wall showers.

There are two Fortress Residences, the ultimate in sensual living spaces and both are located on the upper floor of The Fortress. Each has two bedrooms and two bathrooms, a separate living area, entertainment area and outdoor dining deck and a private cantilevered infinity edge pool with magnificent views of the coastline. Each residence is attended by a 24-hour personal butler, catering to guests' every whim.

The Fortress's sense of design extends to their culinary art with a number of venues serving Sri Lankan cuisine, innovative international fare and Fortress cocktails. And at T, a tea taster will guide guests through the extensive array of teas sourced from the country's lowlands to its hills. Alternatively, partake in one of the hotel's indulgent modern high teas.

The Presidential Villa sets new luxury standards for VVIPs, featuring a large private garden with ornamental ponds, a 330 square metre pool and a sunken dining pavilion.

Banyan Tree Sanya

Hainan Island, China

A perfect setting to restore your *chi*

Set beside white sands, turquoise seas, azure skies and verdant hills and in a climate described as 'endless summer', Hainan's Banyan Tree Sanya is an extraordinary innovation for China – a haven of sun-kissed luxury in an entirely unspoilt and exotic environment.

Spa treatments are available in the privacy of guests' villas.

www.banyantree.com

Our recommendation
The Presidential Villa Complex from $21,800 per night
Spa Pool Villa from $2,560 per night

Best time to visit	**All year round**
Design style	**Chinese with tropical island style**
Architects and designers	**Architrave Design and Planning**
Affiliation	**Banyan Tree Hotels and Resorts**

Water is a key feature of this first all-pool villa resort in China.

Hainan Island is China's second largest island and also its smallest province and is still relatively unexplored. It enjoys white sandy beaches, coral reefs and year-round sunshine, which is why it is often compared to Hawaii and therefore attracts China's wealthy elite. It is no surprise that with all the ingredients of a luxury destination, Banyan Tree chose Hainan Island for a brand new sub-tropical hideaway. Located at Luhuitou Bay on the southern coast of the island, Banyan Tree Sanya is the first all-pool villa resort in China.

Unprecedented in both scale and luxury the resort has spacious and contemporary Spa Pool Villas constructed with local red clay-tiled roofs and black slate-clad walls, combining delightful Chinese detail with a distinctive tropical minimalism. Each villa is fringed with palm trees and lotus ponds enclosed within a private courtyard and there is an outdoor shower and private jet-pool to bask in.

A Presidential Villa Complex comprises two king-sized bedrooms and four adjacent bedrooms with every amenity required by a head of state and the seriously affluent. Everything is on a presidential scale – the extensive reception room, presidential dining room, reception room, theatre, games room, steam with sauna room and gym as well as a 300 square metre swimming pool with outdoor sunken pavilion and heated jet-pool. Of course, comprehensive 24-hour security and valet services are provided for distinguished guests when they are in residence at the Complex. For those with an entourage, up to 44 staff can be housed in the dedicated living quarters which has its own swimming pool, lounge, sauna and steam showers.

The Spa Pool Villas are spread over two levels and set amid a sculptured garden. These are designed for those who desire the luxury of space and privacy – the second floor has an outdoor massage area with twin beds and loungers and an outdoor shower to while away the day. The Spa Pool Villa provides guests with a private 50 square metre pool, heated jet pool and an outdoor bathtub set in a lotus pond. This is a lavish escape from the hubbub of the city.

The resort comes with a signature Banyan Tree Spa and Hydrotherapy Complex with a Vitality Pool and Hydrotherapy Cabin. The Spa features include eight treatment pavilions with two treatment areas each. There is an Affusion shower room, a Thai massage area, two outdoor baths and two steam showers.

The surrounding sea is impressively clean and the reefs offer great snorkelling.

Traditional Chinese architecture and contemporary design details fuse in the interiors of all 61 pool villas of the resort.

Venture outside the resort and sample the island's natural wonders. Tianya Haijiao or 'Edge of the Earth' is a dazzling cape 24 kilometres west of Sanya and where the rocks are covered with love poems carved by those exiled for offending the Emperor. In the island's interior, thick canopies of lush, verdant forest and rolling hills are home to abundant wildlife and plants. Around the island, excellent golf courses boarder palm-fringed beaches and Hainan is home to the South Column Rock, which is featured on China's two-yuan banknote.

Fuchun Resort

Hangzhou, China

Sublime design in harmony with the natural world

Inspired by a 700-year old painting *Dwelling in the Fuchun Mountains*, Fuchun Resort beautifully encapsulates the areas' dream-like quality. Situated southwest of Shanghai in the heart of lush tea plantations and the misty Hangzhou Mountains, it is an exclusive, elegant and refined, luxury lakeside pavilion, a haven of tranquillity amid gentle surroundings.

Enchanting lakeside pavilions on the edge of the mirror-still lake set beside misty tea-covered hills.

www.slh.com/fuchun

Our recommendation
A Fuchun villa with private pool from $2,900 per night

Best time to visit	**March to June and September to January – avoid Chinese New Year and July and August, which are particularly humid months**
Design style	**14th-century Chinese idyll with modern touches**
Architects and designers	**Jean-Michael Gathy, Amanresorts**
Affiliation	**Small Luxury Hotels of the World**

Fuchun Villas enjoy private terraces, Jacuzzi and pool.

Fuchun Resort is not only famous for its serenity, it also boasts one of the finest golf courses in China. Award-winning, the course is extremely challenging and has an excellent driving range for practice and a first-class club house with every amenity. Let the concierge team book you a 'tee off' time or a lesson with the 'pro'.

The experience

Excursions from Fuchun Resort take on the magical quality of journeys to another world. Follow the mighty Fuchun River and explore Hangzhou, capital of Zhejiang province and its political, economic and cultural heart. Walk around the West Lake, which gives the city its shape and purpose, and discover some of the 400 teahouses placed under landmark protection, pagodas, palaces and temples interspersed with Gucci, Hermès and Ralph Lauren stores! A visit to the glorious Six Harmonies Pagoda and the silk museum is a must, and insist on being taken to the grounds of the ancient Tao temple.

Back at the resort, after a leisurely stroll along any of the myriad paths that weave across the estate, take a respite at Lake Lounge and enjoy the awe-inspiring views as you sip your favourite cocktail.

Asian Corner is the in-house restaurant where the chef skilfully prepares local Hangzhou specialities such as lake fish marinated in yellow rice wine, so tender it can be eaten with a spoon.

A stunning state-of-the-art spa features the total range of signature treatments and prides itself on excellent, locally sourced ingredients in its 100 per cent natural and botanical blended pure organic products. Also provided are Himalayan Yoga sessions in the early morning and in the cool of the evening and Tai Chi by the lake – an excellent mental and physical work out.

For your eyes only

Book a Fuchun Villa – residential-style complete with private indoor swimming pool. Luxurious rooms are appointed in elegant contemporary Chinese style combining warm wood and exposed stone. Vast bathrooms are plentifully stocked with local products for sessions of sheer self-indulgence. These villas are unusually large, their high ceilings making them particularly light, airy and cool. On your private terrace recline on a day bed and gaze hypnotised at the glassy mountain lake, its surface broken only by occasional ripples as a fish breaks the water, a leaf shivers down off its willow tree branch, or by the rare rude interruption of a golf ball hit off course.

While Asian Corner, on the pool level, is famous for its Hangzhou specialities, lake-view Club 8 serves an international cuisine.

Fuchun boasts one of the best 18-hole courses in Asia, set among tea plantations. Back from sightseeing, guests can relax in the indoor pool.

Traditional powdered Japanese green tea is served in the Furyuan tea-ceremony room.

Otaru Ryotei Kuramure

Hokkaido, Japan

Merges ancient ideas with concepts from Modernism

Therapeutically located beside a babbling brook in the hot springs valley of Otaru Asarigawa, an hour from some of the best skiing in Japan and only 40 minutes from Sapporo, Kuramure provides a relaxing and spiritually enriching experience of *onsen ryoken* – the ancient form of Japanese retreat where guests soak in hot spring baths while feasting their eyes on a glorious view of the outdoors in remote and natural settings.

www.kuramure.com

Our recommendation
One of the 19 guest suites from $ 342 per night

Best time to visit	**September to end June**
Design style	**Seamless fusion of traditional Japanese warehouse, architecture and modern design**
Architects and designers	**Makoto Nakayama**

Each of the 19 guest suites is individually furnished and consists of a living room and two bedrooms.

Modern in design and conception Otaru Ryotei Kuramure's construction is surprisingly simple, incorporating natural Japanese materials such as timber, earth, paper, bamboo, grass and cloth.

Lighting is subdued and the atmosphere is one of stateliness and oriental composure – a perfect fusion of Modernism with Otaru's traditional Japanese warehouse architecture. Having stepped over the threshold through a heavy stained wooden portal, guests are greeted by electronic glass doors that slide open automatically to reveal the lobby with its Mies-inspired rectangular sofas with rugs and cushions made of leather shreds, juxtaposed with old-style *Ito-koshi*, a fine latticework characteristic of Kyoto.

There are 19 guest suites, all of which are individually decorated and furnished with rice-paper screen, pale wood staircases, tatami rugs and Japanese antiques from the Yi and Ming Dynasties. Every suite has a spacious granite bathroom offering private natural hot spring bathing. Simply throw open the bathroom window and step out into the rectangular pool and into an incredible natural hot spring in your own private oriental garden. This bathing space captures the quintessence of the landscape and the elemental

quality in this *onsen* water. Admire the tree-covered slope of the hillside beyond and the sounds of the brook through a haze of steam rising from the hot spring water as you savour the joys of this relaxing ritual Japanese bath.

For your eyes only
In your room you will find a *samue* (traditional Japanese home wear) and a *hanten* jacket for lounging around. Pamper yourself – bathrooms are stacked with products to cleanse, refresh and rejuvenate.

Kuramure is not only justly famous for its spring water, its cuisine is also renowned. The food reflects Otaru's seaside presence. Dining here is a decadent and drawn-out affair in one of 19 independent dining rooms. Only the choicest ingredients are used to provide innovatively creative dishes: marinated lotus root and whelk, sea urchin custard in broth and langoustine sashimi are just some of the unusual delicacies prepared for discerning palates. Expect 10 delicate courses served on exquisite lacquered trays on which sits beautiful, locally made ceramic ware.

After a languid soak in both an indoor and outdoor pool, why not attend your own traditional green tea ceremony in the Furyuan tea-ceremony room.

A boutique hot spring ryokan *is a nurturing environment with spring-fed indoor and outdoor pools.*

Japanese antiques and occasional Yi and Ming Dynasty pieces from Korea appear throughout the hotel.

Qualia
Hamilton Island, Australia

A world class sensory experience

Nestled into the secluded side of Hamilton Island in a sun-drenched location, fragrant with the scent of eucalyptus carried on a Coral Sea breeze, qualia is an Australian jewel, a unique expression of the country's hospitality. Crafted from locally sourced timber and stone, it is a place of fine textures and beautiful surfaces exuding a relaxed and gentle calm.

A view of the Coral Sea from a utopian pavilion-designed outpost.

www.qualia.com.au

Our recommendation
The Beach House with separate Guest House from $2,900 per night or a Windward Pavilion from $1,500 per night

Best time to visit	**April to December is the driest season. June to August is whale-watching season**
Design style	**Inspired by nature and harmoniously structured in Australian luxury design-style**
Architects and designers	**Chris Beckingham, architect; Freedman Rembel, interiors; Dennis Nona, art**

The design works like an artful set of snap shots – everywhere you turn the views unfold like picture postcards, with breathtaking consistency.

From the moment your foot touches the tarmac in this stylish and elegant resort your only task is to absorb the outstanding natural beauty and the island's wonderful flora and fauna, as staff are eager to assist in every way possible to ensure that your stay is entirely stress free.

Each of the west-facing Windward Pavilions is elegantly appointed and equipped with its own private infinity plunge pool. Lean over and marvel at the breathtaking views of the north-eastern edge of Hamilton Island and the vista of the Coral Sea, the 74 Whitsunday Islands and the magnificence of the Great Barrier Reef.

Fine dining is to be had at the Long Pavilion, a dramatic granite structure with a wall of sliding glass panels and wooden floors overlooking the bay. The restaurant is home to qualia's signature degustation menu – seven delectable courses accompanied by the resident sommelier's wine recommendations. A more relaxed food experience is to be found at Pebble Beach on the water's edge. qualia's Executive Chef oversees an exceptional range of delicious, modern Australian dishes at both restaurants, where you can also sip superlative wines or innovative cocktails – definitely worth a try are the surprisingly strong lychee and green-apple mojitos.

For your eyes only

Treat your senses at Spa qualia. Set in a grove of ancient frangipani trees, it offers unique treatments based on ancient hot-stone massage techniques. Try the Bularri Yarrul, a hot stone massage using 300 million year old stones and Spa qualia's Anoint range of hand-made essential oils.

The Beach House is the ultimate in secluded hideaways. Views from the master bedroom and ensuite bathroom (complete with indoor and outdoor rain showers) will take your breath away as will the huge entertaining area and dining room – seat 10 of your favourite people or let the staff arrange a private banquet just for two. The interiors open up onto the lounge deck which is perfect for watching bird life and the turtles feeding in the morning and afternoon. Of course, there's your own, full-sized swimming pool as well as a separate guesthouse.

Charter a yacht and have the crew take you out on to the Great Barrier Reef for a snorkelling or diving trip, armed with a delicious picnic from the chef. Or let the team organise a private helicopter trip and get a bird's eye view of the Whitsundays and the Great Barrier Reef. Alternatively, make full use of your personal golf buggy to ride around and explore the island.

Totally immersed in the sights and sounds of the bush, the African-style lodge has private decks overlooking the wilderness.

Bamurru Plains

Northern Territory, Australia

Wild bush luxury at the Top End of Australia

A working buffalo station with strong environmental credentials, Bamurru Plains is situated in an animal and bird sanctuary in the savannah woodlands and wetlands of the Mary River delta near Kakadu National Park.

Totally immersed in the sights and sounds of the bush, Bamurru Plains is a private and exclusive camp for staying visitors only. Built on stilts, the simple but stylish, spacious and naturally cool bungalows have been designed with privacy and respect for the environment uppermost in mind. The absolute minimum of trees was removed during construction and more than 60 percent of the power used in the camp is solar generated.

Set among the pandanus vegetation on the edge of the wetlands, each bungalow overlooks the wilderness, which is the primary entertainment at this camp: saltwater crocodiles, wild boar, wallabies, flocks of flying foxes, Asian buffalo and a host of other creatures can be seen either with the naked eye or through binoculars. The bedroom, also affording views towards the floodplains through screened wall, has highly comfortable twin or king-sized beds, with top quality linen and three pillow types to choose from. Ensuite large bathrooms wrap around one side and are equipped with high-pressure showers and hot water, native herbs and other locally produced items.

The hub of the camp is the Lodge Building, constructed in a mix of local sustainable hardwood and recycled industrial materials – here guests meet up for excursions and to dine. The front deck features a BBQ fire pit and wet-edge swimming pool with stunning views across the floodplains. There's a covered lounge area to escape the midday heat and a quiet, well stocked library.

Guests can absorb the unique atmosphere of the reserve through a variety of excursions: take a guide and a four-wheeler or, better still, go up in an airboat, skimming low over the floodplain watching the herds of buffalo and spotting crocodile. Alternatively, for a high-rise adventure, have the team organise a helicopter flight to Kakadu National Park for the day or out to Arnhem Land to view an Aboriginal rock-art site.

In the evening over cocktails, enjoy some spectacular Pacific prawns, scallops and crocodile canapés before indulging in a three course affair of delicious and contemporary Australian cuisine produced by chef Michael Zerbes from NSW who skilfully includes native produce such as kangaroo, buffalo and barramundi infused with native herbs and spices.

www.bamurruplains.com

Our recommendation
Each of the nine safari-style luxury bungalows is sensational from $1,600 per night

Best time to visit	**April to September is optimum but also consider February and March during the monsoon season for 'run off' for Barramundi fishing**
	Closed November to end January.
Design style	**African safari-style lodge in northern Australia**
Architects and designers	**Charles Carlow, owner and the team**

Eagles Nest

Bay of Islands, New Zealand

Somewhere between seven stars and heaven

Stunningly located just north of Russell's Flagstaff Hill and sitting atop its own private peninsula overlooking the glorious Bay of Islands, this 75-acre estate offers world-class big game fishing, sailing, diving and kayaking in a subtropical paradise.

This award winning retreat affords a panoramic view across New Zealand's Bay of Islands.

http://eaglesnest.co.nz/

Our recommendation
**The Rahimoana Villa from $29,000 per night,
or Sacred Space from $4,000 per night**

Best time to visit	**All year, but November to end of April are the warmest months**
Design style	**Eclectic international contemporary and a splash of stylish spirit**
Architects and designers	**Simon Carnachan, architect** **Phillip Lindesay and Barney Limm, construction** **Sandra and Daniel Biskind, interiors**

The Rahimoana Villa enjoys integrated smart system, home cinema, hi-fi systems, high-tech office and enhanced security throughout.

Eagles Nest is an exclusive complex with just five ultraluxe, individually appointed properties to choose from, each decorated with original New Zealand artworks, gorgeous furnishing and equipped with home theatre systems. All come with well tended gardens that blend into the natural topography and foliage that lie at the heart of the Eagles Nest experience. For those without a car, transfer to Eagles Nest by helicopter and combine this adventure with a scenic flight around the Bay.

The experience

Each villa is unique. First Light Villa is a romantic villa hideaway for two overlooking breathtaking seascapes with an indoor/outdoor fireplace and sunset deck. The Eyrie has three elegant double bedrooms and overlooks the Bay of Islands and comes with its own horizon edge swimming pool and private spa. Eagle Spirit also has three double bedrooms, a romantic

fireplace and designer kitchen plus its own pool and spa.

The ultimate home from home, sleek and contemporary, Sacred Space is fully equipped with four double bedrooms each with ensuite bathroom. The showcase master bedroom occupies the entire first floor affording incomparable views that take in the heated 20 metre infinity pool, sauna and spa below. There are walk-in wardrobes and a huge bathroom stocked full of local Living Nature indulgences. There is an enormous lounge and dining area with a home movie theatre and a dream kitchen for in-house dining.

A host of sport and recreational activities can be organised on site for you. However, should you really feel the need to leave the nest for a while, follow the team recommendations and visit one of the local wineries or gourmet restaurants.

For your eyes only

Book the Rahimoana Villa, which means 'Sun God over the Ocean' in Maori – it truly lives up to its name. Wonder at its 320 degree views of the Bay of Islands, the lush and verdant green slopes of the Waitangi and the sight of the Hole in the Rock across the northeast of the Bay.

Taking its cue from the nature around, this state-of-the-art villa is an award-winning architectural and design feat in the palest of grey concrete with granite flooring and glass and steel fixtures, its arresting copper roof shaped like an aeroplane wing, tapered to a fine edge giving it the appearance of floating. Guests have their own private beach, a 25-metre heated infinity pool, Jacuzzi and sauna. Take a drive – a Porsche Cayenne Turbo is at your sole disposal. A dedicated team is on hand to look after you throughout your visit, including personal spa therapists whose services are yours only, as and when required. A personal trainer, a housekeeper and a butler work together to ensure you want for nothing.

The design inspiration for the villas came from the wing of a plane ready for take off.

To boldly go:

The Future is Now

Serrenia

Red Sea, Egypt

An exclusive and architecturally inspired
waterside haven on the Red Sea

Following the wisdom of the ancients who believed that water was not only
the key to life, but integral to their art and culture, Serrenia uses water as
an overarching influence in its design. Here cascades, lagoons and canals all
lead to the spiritual heart of the complex, its spa, set to become a premier
international destination.

www.serrenia.com

Location
**Sahl Hasheesh between the Red
Sea and the Eastern Sahara, Egypt**

Current status
Completion due 2010

Potential
**$3 billion luxury lifestyle
development set in 2.5 million
square metres. Palace residences,
villas and apartments set in an
extensive landscape. A 7 star
hotel, a premier ESPA spa, an 18-
hole golf course and a 330-berth
marina.**

Architects and designers
Foster + Partners

The heat and desert winds influenced the curving protective forms of this luxury lifestyle development near Hasheesh bay, featuring a serpentine spa and a hotel mimicking the submarine world.

Serrenia also draws for inspiration on the natural phenomena of the desert dunes and the winds that have formed their shifting undulations for millennia. Here water and foliage unite, bestowing a sense of grace and tranquillity and enabling the architecture to sit discreetly within the landscape .

Each of the beachfront Palace Residences will have a $50 million price tag and sit on its own island with private bridge access. These highly exclusive properties will enjoy nearly 3,800 square metres of living space with 10- metre-high cathedral ceilings, glass tunnel entrances and private pools set in vast landscaped gardens. They will also feature serpentine roofs, floor to ceiling glass walls and cool minimalist interiors.

With chefs on speed dial and a concierge team available to organise private yacht and helicopter charters, personal shoppers or to fly in your guests string of polo ponies, Serrenia is already the benchmark for the future of residential design and an ultraluxe lifestyle choice.

Songjiang Waterworld

Shanghai, China

Where a life force source is captured and harnessed
into pure luxury

Waterworld draws its inspiration from the waters in an area of
outstanding natural beauty with a concept design intended to
harmonise with this eclectic environment.

www.atkinsglobal.com

Location
Songjiang, Shanghai, China

Current status
Estimated completion date: 2012

Potential
400 bed, 5 star resort hotel located in a water-filled quarry 100m deep, with underwater general areas and guestrooms

Architects and designers
Atkins Architecture Group; Martin Jochman, Paul Rice, Hu Yali, Zhang Jian, Ding Fang and Vivian Chen

Award winning designs for Songjiang within a large water filled quarry. Above ground there are the lobby, various restaurants and an extreme sports centre cantilevered over the quarry.

The structure of waterworld cascades down the rock face as a series of terraced hanging gardens. A central vertical atrium connects the quarry base with ground level in the form of a transparent glass waterfall that complements the quarry's natural water features.

Each of the guest rooms on the outside of the main structure will have curved wings enclosing natural atria which utilise the existing rugged rock face with its waterfalls and green vegetation to make it an astoundingly dramatic feature. The 90 metre high rock face of the quarry will be overlooked by guest's balconies and its base will house restaurants and bars, offering dramatic views of the quarry, the surrounding areas and the internal landscaped waterfall.

In keeping with its aquatic theme, the design will showcase water sports facilities as well as venues for extreme sports – rock climbing and bungee jumping cantilevered over the quarry and accessed by lifts that will rise from the water level of the hotel. A leisure complex is planned with swimming pools and an underwater level in which a tropical reef aquarium and a state of the art spa will be the main features.

Songjiang is 45 minutes from Shanghai and located in a county of outstanding natural beauty – a favourite destination for both Chinese and visitors alike.

In Songjiang is the famous Fang Ta, a four-cornered nine-storey pagoda constructed during the Song Dynasty – climb to the top for panoramic views and a great workout for the legs. Nearby sits the mountain of She Shan, home to She Shan cathedral built from 1925 to1935 and the largest Christian church in East Asia. The Huzhu Pagoda is a leaning tower not dissimilar to the Leaning Tower of Pisa; close by is the Songjiang Mosque, completed in 1367 and one of the largest mosques in China featuring a unique blend of Chinese and Middle Eastern architecture.

Side elevations of the main reception area.

Apeiron

7 Star Resort

A futuristic architectural icon
and world-renowned silhouette

Inspired by the words of an ancient Greek cosmologist who mused that 'the beginning of time was an endless, unlimited mass, subject to neither old age nor decay, perpetually yielding fresh materials from which everything we can perceive is derived', Apeiron, meaning 'infinity', was envisaged as an ultraluxurious island resort with over 350 distinctive and unique suites.

www.sybarite-uk.com

Location
Earmarked for The Gulf, probably Dubai

Current status
In design

Potential
A $500 million island resort with 200,000 sq metres of floor area and reaching 185 metres high with a helipad, butterfly sanctuary, garden and pool oasis and 350 luxury suites

Architects and designers
Sybarite, architects and design studio, London

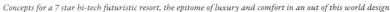

Concepts for a 7 star hi-tech futuristic resort, the epitome of luxury and comfort in an out of this world design

Conceived and designed for construction in water, with access only by yacht or helicopter, Apeiron will be the discerning global tourist's retreat.

Here in a private crescent lagoon, an underwater sculpted landscape of corals and marine plant life will be cultivated to create a surreal world providing views that can be enjoyed from the underwater spa. Above will lie the hotel's private beach with mooring for guests' personal yachts at the heart of the structure. On the 11th floor, an outdoor oasis with views down through the atrium and into the lagoon, will be home to full sized palm trees and fresh water pools. A couple of floors higher and the intention is to build a two floor butterfly jungle and sanctuary, a truly exotic and esoteric – but ultimately, ultraluxe – experience!

To reflect its world-class profile, the hotel will contain luxury brand boutiques, private clubs and cinemas and a number of international restaurants, representing the finest cuisine, wines and spirits from around the world.

When it is built, this fantastic silhouette will become a global architectural icon – instantly recognisable and utterly exclusive.

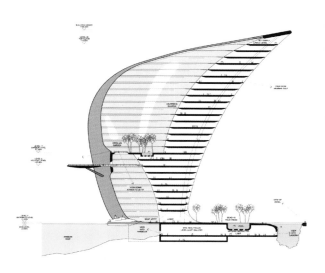

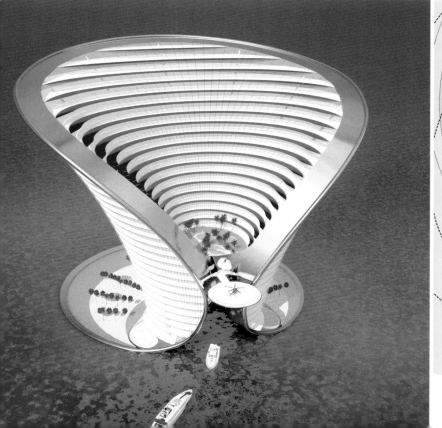

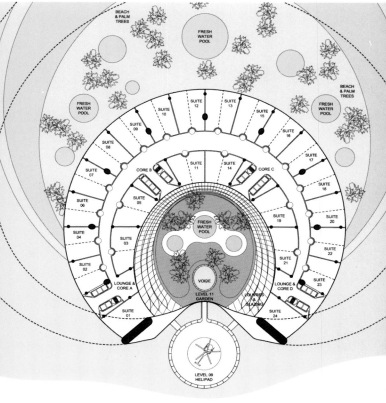

Manned Cloud

The height of luxury floating around the world

Its design has been likened to a flying whale capable of circumnavigating the globe in a matter of days. Its giant rear propeller and two further tilting engines pointing downwards for vertical take-off, this helium powered airship has been conceived as a luxurious floating hotel and an innovative and ecologically friendly mode of accessing spectacular destinations in out of the way locations yet leaving very little impact on the environment.

www.massaud.com

Location
Available worldwide

Current status
In design, hopefully in operation by 2020

Potential
700ft long, 270ft wide and 170ft high. Able to travel 3,100 miles at a height of 18,000ft at a cruising speed of 81mph. Manned Cloud has a top speed of 105mph

Architects and designers
Studio Massaud, and Onera, the French office of aeronautical research

The airship's interior features panoramic viewing decks.

Manned Cloud will gently lift up to 40 passengers into the sky and transport them on a cruising adventure around the world. Each of the private passenger berths will be located on the second level and will be the ultimate rooms with a view – each with a panoramic terrace from which to take photographs or just gaze at the views below.

On the first deck will be the bar and a restaurant providing an eclectic international menu drawing on fresh ingredients that will depend on the location of the airship at the time! A comprehensive library stocked with reference works and periodicals will be complemented by a comfortable lounge for taking tea and a gym for work-outs. There will also be a spa to unwind and relax in during your journey.

Manned Cloud – an extraordinary, eco-friendly airship hotel for the future.

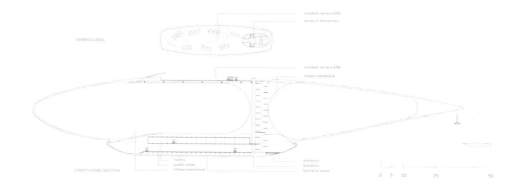

Virgin Galactic

and Spaceport America

Leave earth as a passenger and return as an astronaut

SpaceShipTwo and *WhiteKnightTwo* are Virgin Galactic spacecrafts that will take six guests and two pilots on a two-hour sub-orbital spaceflight out of the atmosphere at over three times the speed of sound and peaking at an altitude of 70 miles. On the trip of a lifetime, spacetravellers will be able to leave their seats to experience about four minutes of weightlessness; they will see first hand the curvature of the Earth wrapped in its fragile, thin ribbon of atmosphere, pick out for themselves planetary detail and gaze awestruck at the vastness of space – to a distance of 1,000 mile in every direction.

www.virgingalactic.com

Location
El Camino Real, New Mexico

Current status
Inaugural commercial flight due 2009

Potential
First commercial suborbital space flights for a ticket price of $200,000 each

Architects and designers
Spaceport: Foster + Partners and SMPC Architects; technology: Paul G. Allen, Vulcan Inc. and Mojave Aerospace Ventures, Burt Rutan, Scaled Composites and Richard Branson, Virgin Group and Virgin Galactic

The sinuous shape of the first private spaceport in the world captures the drama and mystery of space flight itself.

Back on Earth, the New Mexico Spaceport Authority Building is the first private spaceport in the world. Designed to achieve LEED Platinum accreditation, its sinuous shape is dug into the landscape to exploit the thermal mass of the New Mexico climate while interior spaces located around external courtyards cleverly maximise daylight and natural ventilation. Spaceport has been designed to relate to the dimensions of the spacecraft and seeks to capture the drama and mystery of spaceflight itself. It is the operational heart of the venture, the place where the first space tourists will get their initial taste of space travel. Based here are the principal training facilities and functions situated alongside the departure lounge, clubhouse, spacesuit dressing rooms and celebration areas. The canteen and mission control will have east facing views across the runway and landscape beyond.

Visitors and astrotravellers enter the building via a deep channel cut into the landscape which houses a permanent exhibition area documenting the history of space exploration. This channel continues to a galleried level and 'super-hanger' containing the spacecraft and the simulation room.

Tickets are $200,000 each and deposits from over 200 customers around the world have already been taken. It is anticipated that *SpaceShip Two* will be ready to leave Earth's gravitational field for its inaugural commercial flight towards the end of 2009.

Capsule Hotel

Habitats and technology for space and no-space – the Space Hotel of the future

Renowned for its wide range of product design solutions, IS also works for a number of space agencies investigating and testing the materials, technology and design structures that will enable people to live safely in space for extended periods. This is well within the bounds of probability – international space stations have already been orbiting the earth at a distance of some 500km from the surface for a number of years.

www.isspace.com

Designers location
Italy, Florence

Current status
Concept for Space Hotel, Capsule Hotel and Advanced Interior

Potential
IS works also in Product Design and Advanced Architecture

Architects and designers
Company: IS_in and out space_srl
Chiefs: arch. Daniele Bedini and Alessandro Giacomelli
Collaborators:
arch. Edgar Bedini ,
arch. Antonio Fei,
arch. Massimiliano Settimelli

Technology and design for extreme environments.

Inflatable or pneumatic structures are highly flexible interior architectures that can be assembled after launch to create a range of environments, but of particular interest to IS are their potential application as modules for space hotels. IS are developing a module which will inflate to 3.5 x 2.5 metres tall with a porthole to form an authentic hotel room. Currently up to four such modules are in design; they will be attached or hooked onto a space station, itself a rigid structure, to create the space hotel.

After initial testing, it is estimated that the average space holiday will cost $1 million per person. It is anticipated that eight space tourists will arrive by 'space plane' and dock at an arrivals gate with access to the Space Hotel to begin a three to four day orbital holiday in space. Situated inside the rigid core will be the hotel's communal areas: kitchen, dining room, gymnasium and restrooms. Space food entails a limited menu, but the diet will be highly nutritious and the food presented on a fashionable aluminium tray in colour coded packs! It is here in the communal area that a large panoramic viewing window or 'dome' will allow guests to enjoy magisterial views of planet Earth below.

Each of the four private cabins will contain a set of pneumatic furnishings – bed, wardrobe and all other features will inflate as the module itself is inflated. This process is entirely automated and all the technology is now undergoing tests at a variety of space and land enterprises.

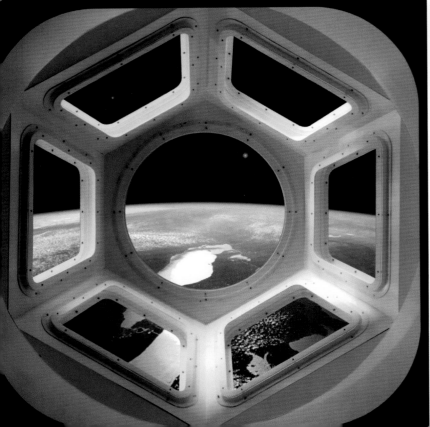

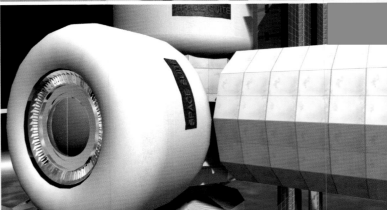

Listings

HOTELS AND ARCHITECTS

Capsule Hotel

www.isspace.com
Architects/designers
Daniele Bedini and Alessandro Giacomelli, IS design company
www.isspace.com

Manned Cloud

www.massaud.com
Architects/designers
Massaud Studio and Onera
www.massaud.com, www.onera.fr

Virgin Galactic

www.virgingalactic.com
El Camino Real, New Mexico
Architects/designers
Spaceport, Foster + Partners and SMPC Architects,
www.smpcarch.com
www.spaceport.org.uk   www.fosterandpartners.com

Australia
Bamurru Plains

www.bamurruplains.com
Suite 9 / Upper Level, Jones Bay Wharf, 26-32 Pirrama Road,
Pyrmont, NSW, 2009 Australia,
Tel. +61 2 9571 6399 | Fax +61 2 9571 6655
info@bamurruplains.com

qualia

www.qualia.com.au
Hamilton Island, QLD 4806, Australia,
Tel. + 61 2 9433 3349
reservations@qualia.com.au
Architects/designers
Chris Beckingham, Freedman Rembel, Dennis Nona
www.freedmanrembel.com

Austria
DO & CO Hotel

www.doco.com/english/index_hotel_eng.htm
Stephansplatz 12, 1010 Vienna,
Tel. +43 01 24 188 | Fax +43 (0)1 24 188-444
hotel@doco.com
Affiliation
Design Hotels
Architects/designers
Hans Hollein, Colin Finnegan,
Gerard Glintmeijer FG Stijl Interiors
www.hollein.com

Bahamas
Musha Cay at Copperfield Bay

www.mushacay.com
Copperfield Bay, Bahamas,
Tel. +1 242 203 602 0300
mushacay@sanctuare.com
Architects/designers
Copperfield Bay Team

Tiamo

www.tiamoresorts.com
South Andros Island, The Bahamas,
Tel. +1 242 471 8087
Architects/designers
Mike and Petagay Hartman

Bahrain
Banyan Tree Al Areen

www.banyantree.com
P.O. Box 75055, Juffair Kingdom of Bahrain,
Tel. + 973 17 84 5000 | Fax + 973 17 84 5001
reservations-bahrain@banyantree.com
Affiliation
Banyan Tree Hotels and Resorts
Architects/designers
Architrave Design and Planning,
http://www.banyantreeresidences.com/aboutus/index.html

Belize
Blancaneaux Lodge

www.blancaneaux.com
Mountain Pine Ridge Reserve, Cayo District, Belize,
Tel. +501 824 4912 | Fax +501 824 4913
info@blancaneaux.com
Architects/designers
Eleanor Coppola and Francis Ford Coppola with Manolo Mestre

Bhutan
Taj Tashi

http://www.tajhotels.com/Leisure/
Post Box No. 524, Samten Lam, Chubachu, Thimphu,
Kingdom of Bhutan, Tel. +975 2 33 66 99 | Fax +975 2 33 66 77
tajtashi.thimphu@tajhotels.com
Affiliation
Taj Hotels Resorts and Palaces

Cambodia
Hôtel De La Paix

www.hoteldelapaixangkor.com
Sivutha Boulevard, Siem Reap, Cambodia,
Tel. + 855 63 966 000 | Fax + 855 63 966 001
info@hoteldelapaixangkor.com
Affiliation
a BMC Management Hotel; Small Luxury Hotels of the World
Architects/designers
www.bensley.com/html/eng/index.html

Canada
The Hazelton Hotel

www.thehazeltonhotel.com
118 Yorkville Avenue, Toronto Ontario, M5R 1C2 Canada,
Tel. +1 416 963 6300 | Fax +1 416 963 6399
reservations@thehazeltonhotel.com
Affiliation
The Leading Hotels of the World
Architects/designers
Architecture: Page + Steele; Interiors: Yabu Pushelberg
www.yabupushelberg.com

Chile
Posada de Mike Rapu

www.explora.com/rapa-nui_thehotel.php
Easter Island, Hanga Roa
info@explora.com
Affiliation
Explora
Architects/designers
Jose Cruz Ovalle

China
Fuchun Resort

http://www.slh.com/fuchun
Fuyang Section, Hangfu Yanjiang Road, Hangzhou, Zhejiang 311401.
China, Tel. +86 571 6346 1111, Toll free 800 525 4800
Affiliation
Small Luxury Hotels of the World
Architects/designers
Jean-Michel Gathy, Amanresorts
www.denniston.com.my/webpagev1/index.html

China

Banyan Tree Sanya

www.banyantree.com
Luhuitou Bay, Luling Road No. 6, Sanya, Hainan Province, China,
Tel. +86 898 88609988 | Fax +86 898 88601188
sanya@banyantree.com
Affiliation
Banyan Tree Hotels and Resorts
Architects/designers
Architrave Design and Planning
www.banyantreeresidences.com/aboutus/index.html

Hotel Côté Cour SL

www.hotelcotecoursl.com
No. 70 Yan Yue Hu Tong, Dong Cheng Qu, Beijing, 100010, China,
Tel. +86 10 65128020 | Fax +86 10 65127295
info@hotelcotecoursl.com
Architects/designers
Shanna Liu

Red Capital Ranch

www.redcapitalclub.com.cn/ranch.html
No. 28 Xiaguandi Village, Yanxi Township, Huairou District,
Beijing 101407, China Tel. +86 10 8401 8886
info@redcapitalclub.com.cn
Architects/designers
Red Capital Group
www.redcapitalclub.com.cn/ranch.html

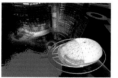

Songjiang Waterworld

www.atkinsdesign.com/html/projects_hotels_songhotel.htm
Songjiang, Shanghai, China
Architects/designers
Atkin's Architecture Group, Martin Jochman, Paul Rice, Hu Yali,
Zhang Jian, Ding Fang and Vivian Chen
www.atkinsglobal.com

Czech Republic

Mandarin Oriental Prague

www.mandarinoriental.com/Prague
Nebovidska 459/1, Mala Strana, 118 00, Prague 1, Czech Republic
Tel. +420 233 088 888 | Fax +420 233 088 668
moprg-reservations@mohg.com
Affiliation
Mandarin Oriental Hotel Group
Architects/designers
Architecture: Dům a město architects Interiors: Rooms: KCA
Interiors; Public areas: Sporer Plus; Spa: Deckelmann Wellness

Egypt

Serrenia

www.serrenia.com
Sahl Hasheesh, Egypt
Architects/designers
Foster + Partners
www.fosterandpartners.com

France

Hôtel Le Meurice

www.lemeurice.com
228 rue de Rivoli, 75001 Paris, France,
Tel. +33 1 44 58 10 10 | Fax +33 1 44 58 10 15
Affiliation
Dorchester Collection
Architects/designers
Philippe Starck and Ara Starck
www.philippe-starck.com/

Hôtel Particulier

www.hotel-particulier-montmartre.com
23, Avenue Junot, 75018 Paris,
Tel. + 33 01 53 41 81 40
hotelparticulier@orange.fr
Affiliation
Hoosta Style Hotels Collection
Architects/designers
Morgane Rousseau and Fréderic Comtet

Great Britain

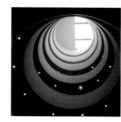

Andaz

www.london.liverpoolstreet.andaz.com
40 Liverpool Street, London EC2M 7QN,
Tel. +44 20 7961 1234 | Fax +44 20 7961 1235
info.londonliv@andaz.com
Affiliation
Hyatt Hotels and Resorts
Architects/designers
Barry Bros, Conran & Partners, John Atkin, Fitch, Wilsdon Design
Associates, Global Hyatt Corporation and JER Partners
www.conranandpartners.com, www.johnatkin.net, www.hyatt

Haymarket Hotel and Townhouse

www.haymarkethotel.co.uk
1 Suffolk Place London SW1Y 4BP,
Tel. +44 20 7470 4000 | Fax +44 20 7470 4004
haymarket@firmdale.com
Affiliation
Firmdale Hotels
Architects/designers
Kit Kemp

Hungary

Lánchíd 19

www.lanchid19hotel.hu
H-1013 Budapest, Lánchíd u. 19-21,
Tel. +36 1 419 1900 | Fax +36 1 419 1919
info@lanchid19hotel.hu
Affiliation
Design Hotels
Architects/designers
Szövetség 39 and NextLab
www.nextlab.hu, www.szovetseg39.blogspot.com

New York Palace

www.boscolohotels.com/eng/hotels/new_york_palace/5star_hotel_
budapest.htm
Erzsébet krt. 9-11, 1073 Budapest,
Tel. +36 1 8866 111 | Fax +36 1 8866 199
reservation@newyork.boscolo.com
Affiliation
Boscolo Luxury Hotels
Architects/designers
Boscolo Hotel Engineering, Maurizio Papiri, ádám Tihanyi D, Simone
Micheli   www.tihanydesign.com, www.simonemicheli.com

India

Baghvan Luxury Wildlife Lodge

www.tajsafaris.com
Baghvan Pench National Park, Village Avarghani, Pench,
Tel. + 91 7695 232829
baghvan.pench@tajhotels.com
Affiliation
CC Africa
Architects/designers
Taj Hotels and CC Africa
www.tajhotels.com, www.ccafrica.com/

The Oberoi Udaivilas

www.udaivilas.com/en-US/Oberoi_Leisure.aspx
The Oberoi, Udaivilas, Udaipur, Rajasthan – 313001, India,
Tel. +91 294 2433300 | Fax +91 294 2433200
gm@oberoi-udaivilas.com
Affiliation
Oberoi Hotels and Resorts
Architects/designers
Parul Jhaveri & Nimish with Lim, Teo and Wilkes
www.designworks.co.nz

The Park

http://newdelhi.theparkhotels.com/
15, Parliament Street, New Delhi, Delhi 110001,
Tel. +91 11 2374 3000 | Fax +91 11 2374 4000
del@theparkhotels.com
Affiliation
Design Hotels
Architects/designers
Conran and Partners, lighting by Paul Cocksedge
www.conranandpartners.com, www.paulcocksedge.co.uk

Ireland

Capella Castlemartyr

www.capellacastlemartyr.com
Capella Castlemartyr, Castlemartyr, County Cork, Ireland,
Tel +353 21 4644050
info.castlemartyr@capellahotels.com
Affiliation
Capella Hotels and Resorts
Architects/designers
MDM, Jack Coughlans Associates, Peter Silling www.jca.ie

Dylan

www.dylan.ie
Eastmoreland Place, Dublin 4,
Tel. +353 1 6603000 | Fax +353 1 6603005
justask@dylan.ie
Affiliation
Fylan Collection
Architects/designers
Spirit & Style and HKD

Italy

Hotel Principe di Savoia

www.hotelprincipedisavoia.com
Piazza della Repubblica 17, 20124 Milan, Italy,
Tel. +39 02 62301 | Fax +39 02 659 5838
reservation@hotelprincipedisavoia.com
Affiliation
Dorchester Collection
Architects/designers
Michael Stelea, HDC Interior Architecture and Design
www.hdc-srl.com/company_profile.html

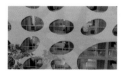

Sixty Hotel

www.sixtyhotel.com
Via Milano 54, Riccione, Italy
Tel +39-0541-697851
reservation@riccione.sixtyhotel.com
Architects/designers
Hotel project: Studio 63 Interiors and furnishing: Wichy Hassan
Affiliation
Design Hotels

Terme Manzi Hotel & Spa

www.termemanzihotel.com
Piazza Bagni, Casamicciola Terme, 80075 Ischia, Napoli, Italy,
Tel. +39 081 994722 | Fax +39 081 900311
info@manziterme.it
Architects/designers
Cesare Luongo

The Gray

www.hotelthegray.com
Via San Raffaele, 6, 20121 Milano, Italy,
Tel. + 39 02 7208951 | Fax +39 02 866526
info.thegray@sinahotels.it
Affiliation
Sina Hotels
Architects/designers
Guido Ciompi

Town House Galleria

www.townhousegalleria.it
Via Silvio Pellico 8, 20121 Milano, Italy,
Tel. +39 02 89058297 | Fax +39 02 89058299
galleria@townhouse.it
Affiliation
The Leading Small Hotels of the World
Architects/designers
Ettore Mocchetti and Italian Institute of Arts

Japan

Mandarin Oriental Tokyo

www.mandarinoriental.com/tokyo
2-1-1 Nihonbashi Muromachi, Chuo-ku, Tokyo 103-0022, Japan,
Tel. +81 (3) 3270 8800 | Fax +81 (3) 3270 8828
Affiliation
Mandarin Oriental Hotel Group
Architects/designers
Cesar Pelli & Associates Architects and Nihon Sekkei Inc., Lim Teo
Wiles Design Works, Nuno Corporation, Nomura Co.
www.mandarinoriental.com

Japan

Otaru Ryotei Kuramure

www.kuramure.com
Asarigawa Onsen 2-685, Otaru, Hokkaidom, 047-0154 Japan,
Tel +81 134 51 5151 | Fax +81 134 51 5000
english@kuramure.com
Architects/designers
Makoto Nakayama

Maldives

Banyan Tree Madivaru

www.banyantree.com
AA. Ethere Madivaru, North Ari Atoll, Republic of Maldives,
Tel. +960 666 0760 | Fax +960 666 0761
madivaru-maldives@banyantree.com
Affiliation
Banyan Tree Hotels and Resorts
Architects/designers
Architrave Design and Planning
http://www.banyantreeresidences.com/aboutus/index.html

Huvafen Fushi

www.huvafenfushi.com
North Male' Atoll, P.O. Box 2017, Republic of Maldives,
Tel. +960 6644 222 | Fax +960 6644 333
info@huvafenfushi.com
Affiliation
Per Aquum Resorts Spas Residences
Architects/designers
Carl Ettensperger, C&C Studio www.ccstudiodesign.com

Morocco

Kasbah Tamadot

www.kasbahtamadot.virgin.com
BP 67, 042150 Asni, Marrakech, Morocco,
Tel. +212 024 368200
Affiliation
Virgin Limited Edition

Namibia

The Fort

www.onguma.com
P.O. Box 6784, Windhoek, Namibia,
Tel. + 264 61 232 009 | Fax + 264 61 222 574
onguma@visionsofafrica.com.na
Affiliation
Visions of Africa Safari Company
Architects/designers
Johann Slee
www.sleeco.com

New Zealand

Eagles Nest

www.eaglesnest.co.nz
60 Tapeka Road, P.O. Box 60, Russell, Bay of Islands, New
Zealand,
Tel. +64 0 9 403 8333 | Fax +64 0 9 403 8880
eagle@eaglesnest.co.nz

Architects/designers
Simon Carnachan, Philip Lindesay and Barney Limm,
Sandra and Daniel Biskind
www.ccca.co.nz, http://heartpower.net

Peru

Inkaterra La Casona

www.inkaterra.com/en/cusco
Plaza Nazarenas 113, Cusco, Peru,
Tel. 0 800 458 7506
sales@inkaterra.com
Affiliation
Inkaterra

Russia

Barvikha Hotel

www.barvikhahotel.com
Barvikha Luxury Village, 8-th km of Rublevo-Uspenskoye shosse,
Tel.: +7 495 225 8880, Fax: +7 495 980 6808
e-mail: info@barvikhahotel.com
Affiliation
The Leading Small Hotels of the World
Architects/designers
Antonio Citterio

South Africa

Phinda Private Game Reserve

www.phinda.com
Kwanzulu-Natal, Tel. +27 11 809 4300
Affiliation
CC Africa
Architects/designers
Ridler Shepherd Louw, Chris Browne, CC Africa
www.ccafrica.com/

Spain

Marqués de Riscal, a Luxury Collection Hotel

www.luxurycollection.com/marquesderiscal
C/ Torrea 1, 01340 Elciego, Álava, Spain,
Tel. +34 945180888 | Fax +34 945180889
reservas.marquesderiscal@luxurycollection.com
Affiliation
Starwood Hotels & Resorts / The Luxury Collection
Architects/designers
Frank O. Gehry
http://www.gehrypartners.com/

Sri Lanka

The Fortress

www.thefortress.lk
P.O. Box 126 Galle, Sri Lanka,
Tel. +94 91 438 0909 | Fax +94 91 438 0338
info@thefortress.lk
Affiliation
Per Aquum Resorts Spas Residences, Small Luxury Hotels of the World
Architects/designers
C&C   www.ccstudiodesign.com

Tanzania

Mnemba Island Lodge

www.mnemba-island.com
Zanzibar, Tanzania
Affiliation
CC Africa
Architects/designers
CC Africa and Chris Browne
http://www.ccafrica.com/

Singita Grumeti Reserves

www.singita.com
Tanzania, Tel. +27 21 683 3424 | Fax +27 21 671 6776
singita@singita.com
Affiliation
Singita
Architects/designers
Wimberly Allison Tong & Goo (WATG)
www.watg.com

United Arab Emirates

Apeiron

http://www.sybarite-uk.com/131.htm
The Gulf, Dubai, UAE
Architects/designers
Sybarite   www.sybarite-uk.com

Burj Al Arab

www.burj-al-arab.com
P.O. Box 74147, Dubai, UAE,
Tel. +971 4 3017777 | Fax +971 4 3017000
BAAfeedback@jumeirah.com
Affiliation
Jumeirah Group
Architects/designers
Tom Wright WS Atkins Architects and Khuan Chew,
KCA International   www.atkinsglobal.com, www.kca-int.com

United Arab Emirates

Desert Palm

www.desertpalm.ae
Al Awir Road, P.O. Box 103635, Dubai, United Arab Emirates
Tel. + 971 4323 8888 | Fax + 971 4323 8053
info@desertpalm.ae
Affiliation
Small Luxury Hotels of the World
Architects/designers
AR+D Singapore architects, IMA interiors Singapore

USA

Gramercy Park Hotel

www.gramercyparkhotel.com
2 Lexington Avenue, New York 10010, USA
Tel. +1 212 920 3300 | Fax +1 212 673 5890
reservations@gramercyparkhotel.com
Architects/designers
Ian Schrager Company
www.ianschragercompany.com

Orchard Garden Hotel

www.theorchardgardenhotel.com
466 Bush Street, San Francisco, California 94108, USA
Tel. +1 415 399 9807 | Fax +1 415 393 9917
mhaney@theorchardgardenhotel.com
Architects/designers
Architecture International
www.arch-intl.com

Sanctuary on Camelback Mountain

www.sanctuaryoncamelback.com
5700 East McDonald Drive, Paradise Valley, Arizona 85253, USA
Toll-free 800 245 2051, Local +1 480 948 2100
info@sanctuaryaz.com
Affiliation
Small Luxury Hotels of the World
Architects/designers
Westroc Hospitality, Allen + Philp Architects
westroc.net/westroc.html, www.allenphilp.com

The Royalton

www.royaltonhotel.com
44 West 44th Street New York, New York 10036, USA
Tel. +1 212 869 4400 | Fax +1 212 869 8965
Affiliation
Morgans Hotel Group
Architects/designers
Roman & Williams, Charlotte Macaux Perelman,
Studio CMP, John McDonald
www.romanandwilliams.com, www.studio-cmp.com

The Setai

www.setai.com 2001 Collins Avenue, Miami, Florida 33139, USA
Tel. + 1 305 520 6000
setai@ghmamericas.com
Affiliation
The Leading Hotels of the World
Architects/designers
Adrian Zecha

Ty Warner Penthouse

www.fourseasons.com/newyorkfs
57 East 57th Street, New York 10022, USA
Tel. +1 212 758 5700 | Fax +1 212 758 5711
Affiliation
Four Seasons Hotels and Resorts
Architects/designers
IM Pei and Peter Marino
www.pcfandp.com, www.petermarinoarchitect.com

Vietnam

The Nam Hai

www.ghmluxuryhotels.com/NamHai.htm
Hamlet 1, Dien Duong Village, Dien Ban District, Quang Nam Province,
Vietnam, Tel. +84 510 940 000 | Fax +84 510 940 999

Affiliation
GHM Luxury Hotels

DEDICATION

To my family, extended family and all my friends whose unconditional love, support and encouragement have enabled me to make my life as rich in experience and as rewarding as it is. This book is for you and in special memory of Michael Newson.

ACKNOWLEDGEMENTS

First and foremost, I wish to thank my editor, Mariangela Palazzi-Williams, for her vision and commitment to *Ultraluxe Hotels*. Without Mariangela's enormous input, talent, enthusiasm and determination this project would never have been realised. Particular thanks go to the excellent copy-editor Lucy Isenberg, and to Roberto Di Filitto and Nathalie Schneider of Spazio8, for the highly sophisticated and elegant design, perfect complement to the subject matter. I would also like to express my deep gratitude to the architects, designers, publicists, hoteliers and everyone who has been so generous in sharing information and supplying photographs and with whom it has been a pleasure to work.

PHOTO CREDITS

The author and the publisher gratefully acknowledge the following for permission to reproduce material in the book. While every effort has been made to contact copyright holders the publisher would be grateful to hear from any copyright holder who is not acknowledged here and will undertake to rectify any errors or omissions in future editions.

l= left, c= centre, r= right, t= top, b= bottom

pp 3, 46-9, 54-7, 212-5 © photos by Banyan Tree; p 4 l courtesy Trump; pp 4 tc, 5 tr, 62-3, 104-7 © Mandarin Oriental Tokyo; pp 4 bc, 230-5 © Eagles Nest; pp 4 tr, 244-5 © Studio Massaud; pp 4 br, 8, 16-21, 250 courtesy Purple PR; pp 5 l, 198-203 courtesy Taj Tashi; pp 5 tc, 34-9, 148-9 © Singita Game Reserves; pp 5 bc, 172-7 courtesy Bacall Associates, Huvafen Fushi; pp 5 br, 82-7 © Marqués de Riscal: a Luxury Collection Hotel; pp 6-7, 208-211 courtesy Bacall Associates, The Fortress; p 9 from left to right: © Hempel Design; © Firmdale Hotels; courtesy Townhouse Galleria; © Mandarin Oriental Tokyo; p 10 from left to right: courtesy Tuckers Point; courtesy Capella Pedregal; courtesy Mondrian; p 11 from left to right: © Burj al Arab; courtesy Town House Galleria; © Marqués de Riscal, a Luxury Collection Hotel; p12 courtesy Royal Olympic; courtesy Nord Light; courtesy Trump; p13 Rien van Rijthven Architecturephotography.org; courtesy Azura, Mozambique; courtesy Virgin Galactic; pp 14-15 courtesy Shutterstock © Emin Kuliyev; pp 22-5 © Four Seasons Hotel New York; pp 26-7 courtesy Musha Cay at Copperfield Bay; pp 28-31 for all the restyling images © François Marechal and Peter Hebeisen, for the Belle Étoile Suite © Hôtel Le Meurice; pp 32-3 © Hotel Principe di Savoia; pp; pp 40-5 courtesy Burj Al Arab; pp 50-3, 166-8 © CC Africa; pp 58-61 © Oberoi Hotels and Resorts; pp 64-9 courtesy Morgans Hotel Group; pp 70-3 © GHM Hotels and Resorts; pp 74-5 courtesy The Hazelton Hotel; pp 76-81 © Firmdale Hotels; pp 82-7 © Marqués de Riscal: a Luxury Collection Hotel; pp 88-91 courtesy Town House Galleria; pp 92-5 © Mandarin Oriental Prague, photos George Apostolidis; pp 96-101 © Boscolo Hotels Hungary; pp102-3 © Barvikha Hotel & Spa; pp 108-9 courtesy Shutterstock © Sean Nel; pp 110-3 © Rien van Rijthven Architecturephotography.org; pp 114-7 courtesy Brighter Group; pp 118-121 courtesy Andaz; pp 122-5 © Hoosta Style Hotels Collection; pp 126-7 © DO & CO Photo Library; pp 128-131 © The Gray; pp 132-3 courtesy Sixty Hotel; pp 134-5 courtesy Lánchíd 19; pp 136-39 © The Park Hotels, India, www.theparkhotels.com; pp 140-3 © Hôtel de la Paix; pp 144-7 courtesy Hotel Côté Cour SL; pp 150-1 courtesy Tiamo Resorts; pp 152-3 © Blancaneaux Lodge; pp 154-5 photos courtesy of Inkaterra; pp 156-9 courtesy Posada de Mike Rapu; pp 160-5 © Onguma Safari camps, photos Dave Rogers; pp 170-1 courtesy Baghvan Luxury Wildlife Lodge; pp 178-181 © Red Capital; pp 182-3, 228-9 © Peter Eve; pp 184-7 © Sanctuary on Camelback Mountain; pp 188-9, p 254 © Capella Castlemartyr; pp 190-1 © Gestione Le Camelie, Manzi Terme Photo Files; pp 192-5 courtesy Kasbah Tamadot; 196-7 courtesy Bacall Associates, Desert Palm; pp 198-203 courtesy Taj Tashi; pp 204-7 courtesy The Nam Hai; pp 216-9 © Fuchun Resort; pp 220-3 © Otaru Ryotei Kuramure; pp 224-7 courtesy Qualia; pp Lucid Design; pp 236-7, 246-7courtesy Virgin Galactic; pp 238-9 © Foster + Partners; pp 240-1 © Atkins; pp 242-3 © Sybarite; pp 248-9 © Daniele Bedini/IS srl.

NOTE TO THE READERS

For consistency, all room rates are given in US dollars and, while every effort has been made to ensure the accuracy of information provided, it is of course subject to change. Readers are advised to contact hotels and resorts for updated information prior to making any travel arrangements.

Dragon stops humming.
"Go away, and play," says
Dragon.
The bees stop humming.
"Go away, and play," say
the bees.
The baby rabbits hop
away.
They hop into the wood.

DRAGON AND THE RABBITS

BY
LUCY KINCAID

ILLUSTRATED BY
ERIC KINCAID

Brimax . Newmarket . England

Dragon lives in the wood.
He hums songs with the
bees.
The baby rabbits want to
hum too. They do not
know how to hum.

Dragon is humming again.
The bees are humming again.
Along comes Mother Rabbit.
"Where are my babies?" says Mother Rabbit.
"I do not know," says Dragon.
"We do not know," say the bees.

Mother Rabbit calls her babies. They do not come. Mother Rabbit begins to cry.

"I have lost my babies," she says.

"Do not cry," says Dragon.

"We will find your babies for you," say the bees.

They all look for the baby
rabbits.
Dragon looks for them.
The bees look for them.
Mother Rabbit looks for
them.
The baby rabbits have
gone.
Nobody can see them.
"They must be hiding,"
says Dragon.

Dragon stops. He stands still.

"Listen," says Dragon. "I can hear something."

"So can I," says Mother Rabbit.

"So can we," say the bees.

Dragon peeps over the
bush.
He can see something.
"Come here," says Dragon.
The bees look over the
bush.
Mother Rabbit looks over
the bush.

The baby rabbits are
sitting on the grass.
"What are they doing?"
say the bees.
The baby rabbits are trying
to hum.
They are trying very hard.
But they cannot do it.

"Hallo!" says Dragon.
"What are you trying to do?"
The baby rabbits see Dragon.
They hop away and hide.
"Come out of there," says Dragon.

The baby rabbits will not come out of the hole. They do not see Mother Rabbit. "Come out of there at once," says Mother Rabbit. "Yes, Mother," say the baby rabbits.

"Come with me," says Mother Rabbit. "We are going home."
The baby rabbits look very sad.
"What were they trying to do?" say the bees.
"They were trying to hum, like us," says Dragon.

"We can show them how
to hum," say the bees.
"Yes," says Dragon.
It takes a long time to
show a rabbit how to hum.
Dragon tries very hard.
So do the bees.
At last they do it.

Dragon is humming.
The bees are humming.
The rabbits are humming.
"I did not know rabbits
could hum," says Owl.
"My babies are the only
rabbits who can," says
Mother Rabbit.

Say these words again

Mother	know
baby	bush
babies	listen
rabbit	trying
once	where
something	show
could	hear